Lessons From the Phantom of the Opera

3rd Edition

by

VICKI HOPKINS

RELEASED JULY 2015

Copyright © 2009 by Vicki Hopkins

ISBN: Softcover 978-0-9832959-5-2

Library of Congress Control Number:
2015910781

All rights reserved. No part of this book may be
reproduced or transmitted in any form or by any
means, electronic or mechanical, including
photocopying, recording, or by any information
storage and retrieval system, without permission
in writing from the copyright owner.

Acknowledgements and Permission to Reprint

HOLY BIBLE, NEW INTERNATIONAL VERSION®.
NIV®. Copyright 1973, 1978, 1984 by International Bible Society.
Used by permission of Zondervan.
All rights reserved.

THE PHANTOM OF THE OPERA
By Gaston Leroux
2002 Modern Library Paperback Edition
Copyright 2002 by Random House, Inc.
Introduction Copyright 2002 by Anne Perry.
Used by Permission

LE FANTÔME DE L'OPÉRA
by
Gaston Leroux
Quotes from the works of Gaston Leroux
Public Domain

THE PHANTOM OF THE OPERA SONG TITLES
From THE PHANTOM OF THE OPERA, Music by Andrew Lloyd Webber, Lyrics by Charles Hart,
Additional Lyrics by Richard Stilgoe
Used by Permission

LOVE NEVER DIES SONG TITLES
From LOVE NEVER DIES, Music by Andrew Lloyd Webber, Lyrics by Glenn Slater, with additional lyrics by Charles Hart
Used by Permission

Table of Contents

Introduction 5

SECTION ONE
CHARACTERS IN PHANTOM OF THE OPERA

Carlotta 11
Christine Daaé 15
Christine as Little Lotte 19
De Chagny Family 22
Erik 26
Joseph Buquet 29
Madame Giry 32
Managers 36
Meg Giry 39
Opera Ghost 42
Philippe de Chagny 45
Piangi 50
Raoul de Chagny 53
The Phantom 58

SECTION TWO
EMOTIONS IN PHANTOM OF THE OPERA

Anger 62
Anguish 66
Confusion 69
Doubt 72
Fear 76
Hate 80

i

Jealousy 84
Loss 87
Love 89
Memories 92
Obsession 94
Passion 97
Seduction..100

SECTION THREE
SYMBOLS IN PHANTOM OF THE OPERA

Angel of Music 104
Box 5 107
Chandelier.. 109
Graveyard...111
Lasso 114
Mask..117
Mirrors.. 120
Music 124
Music Box..127
Red Death..132
Ring...135
Rose...137
Tears 140
Trap Door 144

SECTION FOUR
EVENTS, PLACES & THINGS IN PHANTOM OF THE OPERA

Betrayal...148
Illusion 152

Lair 156
Masquerade 158
Opera! 162

SECTION FIVE
THOUGHTS FROM GASTON LEROUX'S ORIGINAL VERSION

Heaven or Hell 166
Horror 168
Intimidation 170
Lies 172
Morality 174
Poor Unhappy Erik 176
Skeletons, Skulls, and Roses 182

SECTION SIX
THOUGHTS ON LOVE NEVER DIES

Prologue 192
The Phantom in LND 194
Christine Daaé in LND 200
Raoul, Vicomte de Chagny in LND 203
Madame Giry in LND 208
Meg Giry in LND 212

Conclusion 218
Endnotes 219
About the Author 221

Dedication

To the millions of fans who love *The Phantom of the Opera* and share the cry of Erik's heart for unconditional love.

Introduction

"The Opera Ghost really existed. He was not, as was long believed, a creature of the imagination . . ." Gaston Leroux

Gaston Leroux published Fantôme de l'Opéra in 1910. Over one hundred years later, the basic premise of the story is a worldwide phenomenon. Published in a variety of forms and immortalized on stage and film, the story never dies. Writers continue to pen sequels, websites and forums continue to inundate the Internet, literature students dissect its hidden meaning in the classroom, and scholars and psychologists publish commentaries.

Until January of 2008, I ignored the story of *The Phantom of the Opera*. Never required to read the original work in high school or junior college, I only knew it was a story about some creepy man who lived underneath an opera house.

I found no interest in pursuing the literature or watching older film versions. Also, I never attended a stage production in my entire life, so the thought of seeing Webber's play did not enter my mind.

One day while surfing the Internet, I came across a small three-minute clip of the 2004 movie of *The Phantom of the Opera*. My curiosity was finally aroused after watching. I decided to rent the DVD of the Webber - Schumacher movie. Like anyone else, I popped a bag of microwave popcorn, sat on my green recliner in my living room, lifted my leg rest, and pushed play. The next two hours profoundly touched my heart, and I became obsessed with the story. The movie did not satisfy my hunger. I purchased Gaston Leroux's original version, devoured it in a few days, and cried over Erik's pleading words:

"I am not really wicked. Love me and you shall see! All I wanted was to be loved for myself."

After numerous dabs of tissues catching my blubbering tears, I knew I loved the story. It touched the core of my heart. After reading that over 140,000,000 people worldwide have flocked to see *The Phantom of the Opera* on stage since it opened on London in 1986, I felt compelled to write about the characters, emotions, sets, and music that burst with symbolism. Finally, I had the opportunity to see the stage production for the first time in 2009.

Out of a fluke, I started a blog on Google's Blogger entitled, "*Lessons from The Phantom of the Opera*."

(*http://thephantomslessons.blogspot.com*)

When I did so, I did not intend to make a big deal about the site. The blog was a place to dump my thoughts, as most blogs are. I chose the pen name of the *Phantom's Student.* Christine Daaé called the Phantom her great tutor so naturally I became his student. Over 150 posts later, 190,000 hits from 116 countries worldwide, as I pen this introduction, the blog has grown beyond my wildest imaginations.

For me, *The Phantom of the Opera* is a psychological playground. By no means am I a psychologist. I am just a human being having searched my entire life for unconditional love. Redemption and longing for acceptance are the major themes throughout the story, and I believe that is why so many people relate to the Phantom's plight.

I have written *Lessons from The Phantom of the Opera* from my heart. It is how the story reveals itself to me as an average run-of-the-mill fan and contains my own reflections. It is free from the influence of other commentaries regarding its hidden meanings. I have poured my heart into dissecting every morsel of *The Phantom of the Opera* for two years. Where research was required on any particular subject, especially in the area of psychology, I have noted the sources and given credit where credit is due.

Be forewarned that there are Biblical references in my articles because of obvious analogies throughout the story that deal with light and darkness, heaven and hell, and good versus evil. Keep in mind that when the original story was written by Leroux, France was a nation guided by

Catholicism.

My articles touch on the characters, emotions, symbols, and places. I dissect the story from a human standpoint examining all versions, whether it is Gaston Leroux's original work, Webber's stage play or the Webber - Schumacher movie. Some articles are purely informational and include historical background while others examine the driving motivations of the characters. The inspiration for a variety of subjects birthed from my own life experiences. Humor and stark honesty are woven throughout, along with a few personal confessions. In some articles, I have kept my mask on and in others taken it off.

My earlier articles are a bit short, but as time progressed and I became more immersed in Leroux's version, they expanded. You may end up reading posts that are a mishmash of Leroux, Webber's play, and the 2004 movie all in one.

Also, I have added in this third edition my former posts regarding my thoughts on *Love Never Dies*, which is Webber's sequel to *The Phantom of the Opera*. It's been recently announced that it will tour the United States during the 2017-18 season.

I had the opportunity to see the original play performed in London two weeks after opening and then again a year later with some minor changes. After coming home, I posted my thoughts on the characters. If you know nothing about the controversial sequel and do not wish to spoil the experience, I suggest that you skip those posts altogether.

There are other posts in the blog not included

in this book, which I term as "Phantom Ramblings." They can be accessed from the original blog by using the search function. They include:

- Reviews of various Phantom stage productions
- Interview and guest post
- Phantom community matters
- Phantom Fans Week (Las Vegas)

In conclusion, my views and interpretations are not the final word, by any means, and the story may reveal itself to you differently. I am keenly aware that there are many zealous fans of this story, and a few have found fault with my insights. Emotions tend to run high on which version people embrace. Please keep in mind that I have never claimed to be an expert. On the contrary, I'm just another admirer, who had the audacity to put my thoughts on the Internet.

Why am I publishing my blog? It is because my readers expressed the desire to see it in written form. It is my sincere hope you will find more inspiration hidden within the story as you view it through your own opera glasses from Box 5. Happy reading and reflection.

"*I AM LOVED FOR MY OWN SAKE.*"

ERIK, GASTON LEROUX'S LE FANTÔME DE L'OPÉRA

Section One

The Characters

Carlotta
Christine Daaé
Christine as Little Lotte
de Chagny Family
Erik
Joseph Buquet
Madame Giry
Managers
Meg Giry
Opera Ghost
Philippe de Chagny
Piangi
Raoul de Chagny
The Phantom

Carlotta

"... La Carlotta who sings like a squirt..."
Gaston Leroux

Wonderful Carlotta is the Diva of the stage. You could describe her as a tad self-inflated, difficult, overbearing, rude, arrogant, egotistical, and temperamental in nature. These are only a few of her endearing personal qualities. Carlotta is the reigning lead soprano at the Opera Populaire. She has held that position for five years. In Leroux, she is La Carlotta from Spain. In the stage version, she is Carlotta Giudicelli from Italy.

The term "Prima Donna" is an Italian expression for the first lady of the stage. The name carries with it many connotations, most of which are negative in nature. "Diva" is a word that describes a famous female singer. Leading ladies of the opera were viewed as very demanding and high-maintenance individuals, who thought themselves privileged and above others in rank at the opera house.

How did others view Carlotta? Leroux states the Opera Ghost thought Carlotta sang "like a squirt" and "had a common place instrument." He further describes her personality as "celebrated, but a heartless and soulless diva," which probably relates to both her stage presence, as well as her personality.

The Opera Ghost asks the managers why they must continue to cast her when she is past her prime. He recognizes the time has arrived to replace the aging Diva with emerging Christine, and through accidents and mishaps attempts to drive Carlotta from the stage. The Phantom wishes to further Christine's career and warns the Diva not to sing. If she does, something terrible will happen when she opens her mouth. In retribution for ignoring his warnings, along with the managers who allow her to sing the lead in Il Muto, he makes her sound like a toad to embarrass and humble her in front of the audience. After all, she is accustomed to hearing adoring fans yell accolades of bravo. Now the entire audience is laughing at her instead.

She obviously thinks highly of herself in the movie version, but the cast and crew have different views. They stuff their ears with cotton while she rehearses, and a man moons her as she passes by. No one respects her. The managers learn early that to control her behavior they must appease her by pleading. They grovel and shower her with flowers, jewelry, and gifts to satisfy her demands for attention and adoration. One of the managers drinks champagne from her shoe demonstrating the ultimate act of respect, which was a French tradition to honor the presence of a beautiful woman.

Poor Maestro Reyer tolerates the Diva's

commands, and the cast endures her insults and outbursts. Even the movie makes a comedic statement regarding a Diva's personality. Next time you watch the DVD, take a moment to pause the scene in Carlotta's dressing room. Take a closer look at the portrait of Hannibal hanging on the wall, and you will see Andrew Lloyd Webber's head on a platter.

How does Christine view Carlotta? A rival to her aspiring career no doubt. She dreams of the limelight that Carlotta possesses and tastes the adoration of being a first lady, albeit briefly. Her great tutor's purpose is to make her a star. Carlotta, of course, views Christine as competition invading her reigning territory. Do you believe Christine's ultimate success as first lady of the opera would spoil her personality too? It would be interesting to observe how years of success influenced her behavior.

Probably most of us have met someone we would term a Prima Donna or Diva in their own right, even if they do not sing. You know the type—arrogant, rude, difficult, and demanding. There are a few famous singers given the title of Diva due to their personality traits, which match the description of demanding and difficult. Can you think of any?

As we study Carlotta, we see that our Diva possesses an inflated sense of self-worth. In contrast, our dear Opera Ghost possesses a deflated sense of self-worth. Both are at opposite ends of the spectrum, and their sense of worth motivates their behavior. Perhaps Carlotta longed for acceptance and love, and her misguided way of obtaining it came through her obnoxious behavior. On the other hand, Erik longed for acceptance and love, and his misguided way of obtaining it came through violence.

What end of the spectrum do you find yourself? Are you a Diva at heart like Carlotta or a broken spirit like the Opera Ghost? I hope you find yourself somewhere in between.

(POSTED FRIDAY, APRIL 4, 2008)

Christine Daae

"... on that evening, Christine Daaé had revealed her true self..."
Gaston Leroux

Since my original article that I posted on Blogger in March of 2008, my thoughts regarding Christine have changed somewhat. I originally agonized over her character, mostly because of the strong feelings held by fans. Sometimes in forums, such as these, you tend to tiptoe around matters that you think will offend, and I was concerned my thoughts about Christine might not be welcome.

I find Christine hard to analyze. Erik I understand, because I relate to his humanity, pain, and yearning for love. However, I felt somewhat removed from Christine until I took the time to delve further into her background in Leroux's work. You either love or hate her. After all, Christine's decision not to choose Erik is a painful ending in many ways, and fans tend to take the matter to heart over her decision to leave with Raoul.

Christine, as portrayed by Leroux, gives a deeper insight into what makes her tick and sheds light on the motivation behind her actions. The play and movie touch very little upon Christine's past, except to state she is an orphan who came to live and train at the Opera Populaire under the care and guidance of Madame Giry. The story suggests that Gustav Daaé was a famous Swedish violinist and gives him great honor showing a large family crypt in the cemetery. However, in the book, Gustav Daaé was far from rich or famous.

Christine's mother died when she was six years old. Her father devastated over his wife's death, sold their small plot of land and took Christine to the city looking for fame and fortune. Gustav's dream never materialized, and for many years, Christine as a young child was virtually homeless. She followed her father from village to village while he played his fiddle in traveling fairs. If it were not for the kindness of a married couple that came across their path, I believe they would have sunk into obscurity. Professor Valerius and his wife provided housing and education for Christine. They sent her to the conservatory of music, where she learned to excel in her singing skills. In her mid-teens, her father passed away, contrary to the stage version that implies she was orphaned as a small child.

Christine's childhood plays a large role in the choices she makes later in life. Her dependence upon her father is evident, and the longing for a father figure is prominent for many years after his death. Also, having spent much of her childhood wandering the countryside hungry and poor, no doubt plays a huge part in her motivation to seek security and stability elsewhere. In the original work, Raoul's brother, Philippe, insinuates she is merely looking for a rich benefactor to care for her.

The matter of the Phantom is a pivotal point in the life of Christine Daaé. For years, she clings to her father's promise that he would send her the Angel of Music from heaven. When the Phantom begins to tutor her, she believes it the fulfillment of his promise, and the Angel becomes her protector, guide, and in a sense, a father figure. When she learns the Angel is really the Phantom, Christine begins to relate to him as a man. He reveals his human side, which draws her as a young girl emerging into womanhood.

I like the way Schumacher plays that thought throughout the movie, even though some think they are movie bloopers. Frankly, I think they were intentional. When Christine is with the Phantom, she is seductive, attractive, her hair flows freely, her makeup is dark, and her clothing more revealing. Every time she is in his presence, this theme carries throughout the movie and peaks at the "Point of No Return."

After Christine fears the Phantom, she turns to Raoul for protection and security. He becomes her guide, protector, and father figure. Her appearance in Raoul's presence is portrayed as one of innocence and dependence. Her hair is pulled back, her makeup light, her clothing modest, denoting the innocent Christine, who has not emerged into the full sexuality of womanhood.

Christine is on a journey in this story, and that is a journey toward growth and maturity.[1] A critical turning point arrives in her life. Erik stands before her with a noose around Raoul's neck demanding that she make a choice. Up until this time, she's been guided and watched over by her father, Madame Giry, the Angel of Music, and Raoul. Now she is alone, faced with a horrible decision and that decision releases her into adulthood. She finally becomes her own person, not dependent upon another. She chooses her own path. What motivates the decision she makes is another discussion entirely. Her motives could be birthed from fear, compassion, love, personal desires or ambitions. For my opinion on her motives, read my next article on Little Lotte.

I think Christine made the right choice for both her and Erik. Two emotionally incomplete people do not make a happy whole. Erik needed to learn what constitutes true love, and, as a result, he was touched at the core of his humanity by what transpired. In her own way, Christine helped him arrive at that revelation. On the other hand, Christine needed to mature, become her own person and less dependent upon others, thus stepping into adulthood. Erik helped her arrive and cross at that critical turning point.

If the basis for Christine's choice to stay with Erik came from either coercion or dependency, there would be no happiness for either of them. Erik and Christine were both on a journey together—a journey toward wholeness. Where that journey continues to lead them, I leave to your imagination and to the writers who continue to pen sequels about their lives.

(POSTED FRIDAY, MARCH 7, 2008)

Christine as Little Lotte

"Little Lotte thought of everything and nothing."
Andreas Munch

Why did Raoul call Christine by the nickname of Little Lotte? The name originates from a poem entitled, *A Child's First Sorrow* by Andreas Munch[3] a Norwegian poet who lived in the early nineteenth century. Leroux quotes the first verse as follows: "*Little Lotte thought of everything and nothing.*" He changes the remainder of the original verse to read:

"*Her hair was golden as the sun's rays and her soul as clear and blue as her eyes. She wheedled her mother, was kind to her doll, took great care of her frock and her little red shoes and her fiddle, but most of all loved, when she went to sleep, to hear the Angel of Music.*"

Leroux writes her father spoke of the story in front of Raoul, who picked up the name Lotte. Christine's father always wove the tale of the Angel of Music into any story he told, and Leroux revises the original verse from Munch's poem to add the reference to the Angel of Music.

The poem is about a little girl who rescues a bird in the winter time and nurses it back to health. When spring arrives, the bird wants to leave and fly away, but Lotte keeps the bird not realizing it wishes for freedom. One morning when she arrives to feed the bird, she finds it dead at the bottom of the cage, which becomes the little girl's first introduction to sorrow and grief in life.

"*The sweet childhood blush faded from her cheeks, and slowly from her heart a dark pain rose. She could not know, what this pain was; but sorrow had written its first rune in her heart. And marked its image deep on her soft features. No longer did it disappear with her last tear.*"

The death of her father profoundly changed her outlook on life. Christine, as we all know, grieves for quite some time and is fixated with the memory of her dead father. I find the last few verses of the poem revealing, especially the verse that death, "*marked its image deep on her soft features.*"

Beyond the poem, I think it is safe to assume that Christine's childhood had a profound effect on her decisions regarding the matter of Erik and Raoul. Think about these scenarios. Christine grew up in a world of poverty, and Raoul offered her a world of wealth. Christine is an orphan, but when she marries Raoul, she is suddenly part of a large family. Finally able to release her fixation on her dead father, she replaces it with the security she finds in Raoul.

On the other hand, look at what she would face in a life with Erik. Christine would return to an existence filled with insecurity and possibly danger. She would once again be isolated from the world and left in social poverty. Like Erik, she would be an orphan again, without family or a sense of belonging.

What else can you glean from the poem above about the poor bird locked in a cage that died in captivity? I suppose that if you dig deep enough, you might find symbolism in that morsel as well, especially if you equate Christine as the little bird locked in a cage.

(POSTED FRIDAY, NOVEMBER 28, 2008)

DeChagny Family

". . . one of the oldest and most distinguished families in France, whose arms dated back to the fourteenth century."
Gaston Leroux

Who are these people? Well, it depends on what storyline you choose—Webber or Leroux.

In the stage play, Raoul is the patron of the Opera Populaire, a financial and artistic supporter of the operatic arts, along with his parents who hold titles of nobility. By virtue of Raoul's title, Vicomte, his father holds the title of Comte over him, and there is no mention of siblings.

In the original work, Raoul's parents are not alive, contrary to Webber's version. Leroux indicates Raoul's mother died giving him birth. At the age of twelve, his father passed away, and his two sisters and elder brother, Philippe, raised him. Raoul also spends time with his aunt, and while visiting her seaside home, he meets Christine.

The de Chagny family, as written by Leroux, is a well-established family dating back to the fourteenth century, holding a vast amount of property and wealth. They have their own family box at the opera house to view performances, and it is not Box 5. The characters of Raoul and Philippe, as aptly penned by Leroux, give further insight into these individuals. For those of you who have never read Leroux, here are few tidbits of character background.

Raoul was noted as being extremely polite and a perfect gentleman in his behavior but somewhat shy. He had a tendency toward openly showing his emotions. He loved the sea, and one of his ancestors was a famous naval admiral. Raoul graduated from the French Naval Academy with honors, and at the time of the Phantom matter, was on a long furlough. His physical appearance is described as a charming twenty-one-year-old, but looking much younger, possessing a fair, perfect complexion, blue eyes, and a small mustache.

Philippe de Chagny was his elder brother by twenty years and spoiled Raoul. He was proud of his achievements in the Navy. Leroux's description of Philippe's character is as follows:

"*Philippe Georges Marie Comte de Chagny was just forty-one years of age. He was a great aristocrat and a good-looking man, above middle height and with attractive features, in spite of his hard forehead and his rather cold eyes. He was exquisitely polite to the women and a little haughty to the men, who did not always forgive him for his successes in society. He had an excellent heart and an irreproachable conscience.*"

Philippe de Chagny's dead body is discovered near the Phantom's lake, and there is speculation that he died at the hand of Erik though he insists it was an accident.

How did the de Chagny's view Christine Daaé? Philippe often fought with Raoul over his affections for the young lady. Raoul's brother termed her as "little baggage." He insinuated that because she was alone in life, had no protector or benefactor, she wanted more from Raoul and sought only his title and money.

Raoul, of course, loved Christine from the moment he met her at the sea and rescued her red scarf when it blew away and fell into the water. After spending the summer together, they became childhood sweethearts. He returned home but did not see her again until three years later.

It's interesting to note Leroux pens that when they meet again, Raoul declares upon leaving that he would never forget her. But he, *". . . went away regretting his words, for he knew that Christine could not be the wife of the Vicomte de Chagny."*

Why did he say such a statement? In the time in which they lived, both family and society objected to the marital match because of their difference in class. He was a titled Vicomte, and Christine was a commoner. Even Christine knew the obstacles, for she later states to Raoul, "*Whatever happened, your position in society forbade me to contemplate the possibility of ever marrying you.*"

The more time I take to study Raoul's character in depth, the more I appreciate the man. Even though many fans prefer that Erik and Christine live happily ever after, some fans dream of Raoul and Christine. Once you understand the man behind the character, you have to give him some credit. He worshiped the ground she walked on and risked everything to be with the woman he loved. In the book, he dares to defy his brother's wishes because he longed to marry her. In both versions, he risks his life to save her from the Phantom.

So is the story real or fantasy? Was it possible for Raoul and Christine to live happily ever after in nineteenth century Paris? You might want to think that matter over because no doubt there were great obstacles to their match had they wed.

As always, I encourage you to pick up the original version and read. It will give you a deeper understanding of the characters and their motivations.

(POSTED SATURDAY, DECEMBER 6, 2008)

Erik

"All I ever wanted was to be loved for myself."
Gaston Leroux

In this article, let's take a deeper look at Erik—not the Phantom of the Opera (his disguise) or the Opera Ghost (his persona), but the human part of the man behind the mask. The person that we identify with, which is the man and his humanity. In Leroux's book, he is known as Erik; in Webber's version his real name is never mentioned or used.

Anne Perry, in her introduction to Leroux's version, published by Random House, describes Erik as, "*...the best and the worst in all of us. He is all of us who have ever walked alone, and hated themselves, and longed for redemption.*"

Erik is a tortured soul with a mind and heart in agony. He is wounded and broken within but radiates a hardened exterior to mask his pain. No one gives him compassion, and, as a result, his heart has become dark and violent. He lives a life in isolation, hidden in the shadows and untouched by the warmth of another human being. Erik is unloved and unwanted. He dreams of beauty and secretly yearns for heaven but lives in perpetual hell. He hates himself, equating his existence to a gargoyle of a man doomed to a life of loneliness.

He wants Christine to learn to love the monster behind the mask. He longs for acceptance. He pleads with Christine to save him from solitude. When she exposes him, he resorts to force to obtain what he needs and wants from her because he is convinced no one can love a deformed and ugly man. He is so desperate to free himself from a lonely existence that he will do anything to make his inner pain leave, even if it means kidnap and murder. His face reflects the two warring personalities that dwell within his soul—light and darkness. He cries for redemption and love.

Of all the characters in *The Phantom of the Opera*, we gravitate toward Erik. We relate to his solitude. We feel his pain because we have perhaps tasted the bitterness ourselves. We want to embrace him and give the love he hungers for because we long for it as well.

Even with all the darkness he embodies as the Phantom, we forgive his indiscretions because we understand what motivates the beast within him, driving him to do the unthinkable. We also, like Erik, secretly yearn for heaven. Like him, we have the dark capacity within us to resort to the unconceivable in our search for love. We too are skilled in hardening our exteriors to mask the pain within our hearts. We long for redemption.[2]

Loneliness and isolation are a human condition that touches many lives, and this is Erik's humanity. Research confirms that we need companionship, love, and touch to be healthy and whole. We are moved by Erik's humanity because he represents a basic need we all share, which is to be fully known, loved, and accepted for who we truly are.

As Christine sang to Erik that God grant her courage, may we find the capacity in our hearts to give to other human beings the gift of unconditional love. I believe that is the message of *The Phantom of the Opera* so we can grant compassion to those who need it.

(POSTED MONDAY, FEBRUARY 18, 2008).

Joseph Buquet

*"But the announcement of the death of Joseph Buquet had
served them as a brutal reminder . . . "*
Gaston Leroux

Now we have Joseph Buquet, a wretched man, and disgusting looking individual. He is the resident opera house drunkard, stalker, and peeping Tom. He has the distinction of becoming the victim of the Phantom's revenge, hung dead from the end of a taut rope.

Why has the Phantom chosen Joseph Buquet as his target? Did he speak too often of the Ghost? Make one too many jokes about his appearance and existence? Did OG think the time had arrived to silence him? Even Madame Giry warns Buquet that silence is prudent.

An interesting human behavior we see displayed or have sunken to its depths ourselves, is that we tend to judge others harshly on character flaws we also possess. We have heard shocking news stories about high profile individuals caught in some sin or weakness. Usually before their own downfall, they have publicly attacked or defamed another individual with the same flaw.

Joseph Buquet is obsessed with the chorus girls, peeking at them dressing and undressing, stalking and watching them in the darkness. Our Opera Ghost seems to possess a similar problem, only in slightly different proportions. He's obsessed with Christine, daydreams about her, watches her, and stalks her from the darkness.

Yet the Phantom throws a noose around Joseph Buquet's neck and strangles the life out of him dropping him from the scaffolding for all to behold his twitching body at the end of a rope. He stands vindicated above, as he watches his limp body fall to the stage floor. Frankly, I thought the actor in the movie version portrayed the strangulation scene quite well. It was effective enough to see the morbid enjoyment in the Phantom's eyes while strangling the life out of the poor man. It gave me the shivers.

What wretchedness did the Phantom see in Joseph Buquet that made him strangle the life out of the poor guy anyway? Sure, he was a drunkard and a peeping Tom but was his crime worthy of the death sentence? Did the Phantom see a glimpse of his own personality in the wretched man he despised? The Phantom shows no compassion or forgiveness for Buquet's flaws though he yearns for compassion and redemption himself. Of course, at this stage in Erik's life, he has never experienced compassion. It's simply not in his soul to offer what he doesn't understand.

That's usually our problem when we judge others too harshly for flaws, especially when we possess the same ones. We have little compassion but plenty of judgment. Judging others is a means of self-justification.

(POSTED SUNDAY, APRIL 27, 2008)

Madame Giry

*"I absolutely insist upon the good and loyal services of
Madame Giry, my box-keeper."*
Gaston Leroux

Madame Giry, friend to Phantom. In each version of *The Phantom of the Opera*, she's depicted slightly different.

In Leroux, she's an elderly woman, a widow, dressed in a worn-out black taffeta dress, with a dingy hat, whose job is that of the concierge of the patron's boxes. In the stage play, she is ballet mistress, a middle-aged widow, who carries a cane, appearing as a stern ominous woman. In the movie, she is the ballet mistress and choreographer, a middle-aged widow, carries a cane, but possesses less of an overbearing character. All versions have Meg as her daughter, a talented ballet dancer.

Each of these portrayals, however, focuses on her personal knowledge of the Opera Ghost. She is his messenger and accomplice in many ways. Madame Giry collects his salary, delivers his notes, informs others when the Opera Ghost is well pleased, warns of his displeasure and capability of violence, and delivers roses to Christine. When others dare to go against Erik's wishes, she knows nothing good can come of their decision. She warns Joseph Buquet to keep quiet about what he knows and not to enrage OG by his actions, but her warning goes unheeded.

As far as the Phantom's origination, in Leroux there is no indication that she is aware of his past. In the play, she becomes acquainted with Erik as a circus freak, who escapes and hides at the opera house. In the movie, she is his sole rescuer from the traveling fair, and the one who hides him from the world and its cruelties. She admires him as a genius, architect, magician, musician, and composer.

Madame Giry brings Christine to live at the opera house upon her father's death and treats her like a daughter. When Carlotta storms off the stage, she seems to know it is the opportune time to introduce Christine's talent, no doubt at the prodding of OG. She is aware that he has tutored her, and she is ripe and ready for her debut performance. She is also aware of the Phantom's fascination with her as a woman. She watches him lock Christine's dressing room door without protest, knowing fully well his intentions. On the other hand, when the Phantom in his madness kidnaps Christine and destroys the opera house in a fire, she befriends Raoul showing him the way to the lair.

Madame Giry is a friend to the Phantom and knows his secrets. She is his rescuer, enabler, accomplice and is sympathetic to his plight. The Phantom trusts her and no doubt uses that trust to his advantage to carry out his desires. However, he protects her and Meg from harm and oversees their wellbeing throughout his residence at the opera house. He deals harshly in Leroux's version with the managers when they attempt to remove her from her post. The Phantom is indebted to Madame Giry for her help, and she obviously respects him, albeit that respect is laced with a healthy dose of fear. Whatever other emotion she feels for him remains speculation.

I view Madame Giry as a rescuer and enabler. Though her actions were well intended, she enables him to live a life hidden from the world. As a result, he never learns to deal emotionally with its cruelties or dares to venture into the world and find a place in society. The opera house is the only world he knows. In a sense, she frees him from the jeers of mankind but binds him to a life of solitude.

Of course, in Leroux, we know the Phantom lives a life elsewhere before coming to the opera house to reside. He served a sultan, built palaces and tortured souls.

I believe in the end, Madame Giry admits the Phantom's madness must stop, and she no longer hides his secrets. He eventually destroys the only world they both know and love.

I confess that I am somewhat of a rescuer and enabler possessing the Madame Giry syndrome. I tend to help others so much it usually leads to their continued lack of growth, as well as to my own detriment. As much as we can care for another human's plight, rescue and enablement are not always the best answers to helping a person grow. It does not promote maturity that leads to self-sufficiency or wholeness. Madame Giry's relationship with Erik is a prime example.

(POSTED SATURDAY, MARCH 29, 2008)

Managers

"My Dear Managers: So it is to be war between us?"
Gaston Leroux

M. Armand Moncharmin and M. Firmin Richard are the new managers. The sign has been hung. "Opera Populaire Under New Management." The retiring owner is leaving, and the new management has arrived to take over the show. For some reason that always carries with it the assumption that new management means better things to come, but that may not necessarily be the case. Our new managers thought they were buying themselves into the world of arts and high society, but little did they know the opera house was haunted!

What does their presence represent in the story of *The Phantom of the Opera*? It's the age-old struggle of control, and it's a struggle that many of our players are staging against one another in the story. *So it is war between us?"* declares the Opera Ghost in Leroux. In the movie, the Phantom declares to Christine and Raoul, "*Let it be war on you both!*" Yes, it is war, everyone struggling for control of territories, hearts, and stardom.

Messrs. Moncharmin and Richard have amassed their fortune in the junk business. They have purchased the opera house from the retiring owner, who, by the way, is leaving because of his health and moving far away. No doubt, the new managers having amassed their fortune suggests they both had humble beginnings. Now having hit the big time, they can buy their way into society's acceptance of the upper class who regularly attend performances.

On the day of their arrival, the retiring manager announces the new ownership and the new managers introduce their new patron, the Vicomte de Chagny. Immediately they face two obstacles. First, they meet controlling Carlotta, who we all know possesses a bit of an attitude problem. She's out to manipulate and control the new managers from the get-go, and they learn early how to grovel and appease her sour personality.

To complicate matters, the Opera Ghost reveals his haunting existence. The managers believe everyone is obsessed. OG drops his welcome note, and Madame Giry reads the message. He has the gall to welcome them to his opera house, proceeds to outline his stipulations for their peaceful existence in his domain, which includes leaving Box 5 empty for his use, and reminds them that his salary is due. You would think OG's owns it all.

The stage is set; it's war! Our Opera Populaire becomes a battleground. Control is at stake. Both claim ownership and the fight begins. Our dear

Phantom struggles to keep his reign, and the new managers struggle to reject his rule. They deem him an insane lunatic, spurn his demands, refuse to pay his salary, give Box 5 to Raoul, and cast Carlotta in Miss Daaé's place.

The Opera Ghost warns them of dire consequences for rejecting his orders and retribution ensues. Carlotta loses her voice, and Joseph Buquet hangs at the end of a rope. As far as OG is concerned, the managers should stay in their offices and leave the arts to him. He ultimately ruins them by destroying the Opera Populaire.

Of course, the entire story contains struggle and control. The managers are against the Opera Ghost, the Opera Ghost against the managers, Raoul against the Phantom, the Phantom against Raoul, and Carlotta nipping at Christine's heels. All of these characters are warring against each other for territorial possession, whether it is the opera house, a woman's heart or stardom.

(POSTED WEDNESDAY, APRIL 16, 2008)

Meg Giry

"I owe it to him that my little Meg was promoted to be the leader of a row."
Gaston Leroux

Probably the most difficult thing I encounter analyzing the story are the different portrayals of the characters found in all three versions: Leroux, the stage play, and movie. There are variations in each, and Meg Giry, the daughter of Madame Giry, is no exception. Referred to as "little" Meg in Leroux, she is also called the, *"most charming star of our admirable corps de ballet."*

In the novel, Leroux describes her as having eyes black, black hair, a dark complexion and being little boned. Perhaps that is where the "little" reference comes in. In the film version, she is opposite, much more beautiful, curvaceous, blonde-haired and blue eyed woman, but still on the petite side. Leroux writes that later in life she becomes the Baroness de Barbazac, perhaps in fulfillment of OG's earlier prophesy to her mother that someday she would be empress.

Meg is aware of the existence of Opera Ghost and has received that knowledge no doubt from her mother. OG apparently helps her career by arranging for her promotion to the leader of a row in the ballet corps. She knows about Box 5 and shares secrets about the Opera Ghost with the other girls in the ballet corps, sometimes to her amusement by frightening them with stories about his existence. She states at one point:

"Awful things! Truly awful. The floor in our dressing room starts to run with blood."

Leroux never mentions that she is a friend to Christine Daaé. She comments in the novel on Christine's ability to sing by stating that before she obtained a divine voice, six months prior she, *"sang like a rusty hinge."* The storyline, of course, in the play is different. She is close friends with Christine, her mother taking her as her own daughter, and the two of them grow up like sisters.

Meg clearly knows more than she is telling Christine about the Opera Ghost. While in the chapel, Meg asks if Christine thinks it is the spirit of her dead father coaching her. Christine replies, "who else?" Meg turns her head, seemingly knowing it is the Phantom. She also appears fascinated with the Phantom while watching his interaction with Christine. If we are to read behind the lines of their friendship, she must know of Christine's love for Raoul and her plans to betray Erik. She wants to run with Raoul as he rescues Christine, but her mother holds her back. In the end, she obviously persists in longing to see where Erik lives, as she is the first to enter the Phantom's lair. She searches for him, finds him absent, but sees his mask and carries it off with her.

To me, the movie portrays Meg as a woman of possibilities beyond the sad ending of the story, perhaps for our benefit and imagination. Book sequels exist that follow that line of thought. It's not difficult to believe that this man, who she has known since childhood as the Phantom of the Opera, did not hold for her as a young woman some mysterious attraction. After all, her mother served him faithfully for years. Perhaps Meg was thankful for his care, or dare I say, in love with Erik.

Meg is a woman of possibilities. Who is Meg to you? If you were Meg, would you follow Erik through the mirror? That's the great thing about fiction—you can write whatever you choose and take the story wherever your imagination wishes to travel.

(POSTED SATURDAY, APRIL 12, 2008)

Opera Ghost

". . . the Opera ghost and the Angel of Music are one and the same person; and his real name is Erik."
Gaston Leroux

The Opera Ghost. Who is he? He is a ghost who wanders about the opera house, a tortured soul, like other ghosts who continue to haunt places they once inhabited. Anne Perry in the introduction to Gaston Leroux's work by Random House terms him a very, *"complex ghost, who loves and hates, who creates and destroys, who plays tricks, writes letters, demands money, who takes terrible revenge, who kills in anger and to protect, and who is tortured beyond endurance."*

The Opera Ghost, as we know him, is Erik's persona.[4] The word persona is a Latin word for "mask" or "character" that a person portrays. It's the self-constructed image Erik chooses to express who he is to the world. He is dead, and he is a ghost. Being a ghost is the role he plays amongst the living. This is how Erik wants the social world to know him.

He prefers you address him as the Opera Ghost or OG. He doesn't use the name Phantom or the Angel of Music. Only those close to Erik enjoy that privilege. He wants you to think he is a ghost. He exists but in a different dimension. After all, he is dead. You cannot see him, but he can see you. He watches you from the shadows when you are unaware. He slips through walls, rooms and disappears. His voice travels as if he is everywhere and anywhere. You cannot see him unless he allows you a fleeting glimpse of something moving in the shadows.

He communicates with the living through his notes. He signs them with the seal of a skull to remind you that he is dead. He oddly uses the phrase that he is your "obedient servant." He communicates in the most amiable and polite nature when you please him, but takes terrible revenge and haunts you when you do not obey his commands. To those who occupy the opera house, he is OG. This is his home, and he wants you to know he haunts it but allows you to remain as his guest only if you do his bidding.

Erik clearly portrays his social standing in life as the walking dead. Even when he attends the masquerade, he appears to the crowd as Red Death stalking abroad. His persona speaks volumes about how he perceives himself among the living. Being a ghost provides anonymity, stealth, and power through intimidation. Your choice is to do his bidding or suffer his wrath.

Erik in his persona is a ghost, wandering about the opera house only known as death. This is his tortured existence and doom throughout eternity. Erik's pain grasps our hearts once again, as we continue to understand the complexity of who he is as a human being. Being a ghost, is another facet of his personality.

What is the image you choose to portray to the world? You may not be a ghost or the walking dead, but there probably is another character you portray that makes you feel safe in social surroundings. Do you have an idea what your persona might be?

(POSTED WEDNESDAY, FEBRUARY 27, 2008)

℘hilippe de Chagny

". . . inexplicable death of Count Philippe . . . "
Gaston Leroux

Dare I write about Comte Philippe de Chagny, the elder of brother of Raoul? (Inhales deeply and picks up quill with shaking hand to find the courage within to tread upon sacred ground.)

Philippe de Chagny is a Comte revered by many in Leroux's original version. He's a man I find everywhere on the Internet. He continues to be written about in Phantom books and sequels. He is played by multiple individuals in roleplay groups around the Internet, and there's even a YouTube video made in his honor.

Here is a short description of his character as penned by Gaston Leroux:

"*Philippe Georges Marie Comte de Chagny was just forty-one years of age. He was a great aristocrat and a good-looking man, above middle height and with attractive features, in spite of his hard forehead and his rather cold eyes. He was exquisitely polite to the women and a little haughty to the men, who did not always forgive him for his successes in society. He had an excellent heart and an irreproachable conscience."*

Philippe, of course, is the head of the de Chagny family. He's inherited from his deceased father a large, prosperous estate containing a great deal of property. His mother passed away at the birth of his younger brother Raoul, and his father passed away when he was thirty-two and Raoul twelve. His life is suddenly thrown into the management of the estate, which Leroux states was "no easy task." Also, he is faced with the duties of raising his younger brother and caring for his two sisters.

The sisters have little mention, but Philippe's relationship with Raoul is expounded upon. He is devoted to his younger brother's education. Philippe spoils him but is very proud and pleased of Raoul's naval career. When Raoul comes home on furlough, he introduces him to Parisian luxuries and delights but makes sure that he does not set a bad example for his younger brother. He's balanced in work and pleasure, and his outward demeanor in public is faultless.

Philippe, however, is opposed to the match between Raoul and Christine Daaé, calling her "little baggage" believing she is only after Raoul's money since she has no benefactor to care for her. Philippe and Raoul argue over the matter often, according to the household servants. Even their disagreements are noted in the local news:

"The two brothers are said to adore each other; but the count is curiously mistaken if he imagines that brotherly love will triumph over love pure and simple."

As a result, the two go head to head. Raoul plans to run away with Christine, and Philippe intends to stop him at all costs. As usual, in the heat of conflict personality traits loom large, and we are able to see what possibly makes this charismatic man tick.

I've already written in former posts that I believe Raoul to be head over heels in love with Christine, so much so he was willing to die to save her life. What about Philippe though? Why is he so hell-bent on stopping the union between his brother and Christine? I came across an interesting quote that I thought fit Philippe quite well.

"There is nothing to which men cling more tenaciously than the privileges of class." (L. Woolf)

Philippe de Chagny comes from an aristocratic world, filled with expectations, and codes of social behavior. Remember, Philippe is twenty years Raoul's senior. His background was no doubt heavily influenced by his father and mother, and the generations of de Chagny's that date back to the fourteenth century. The coat of arms hangs in his residence, along with portraits of ancestors reminding him of the way things have always been done.

Raoul, however, is threatening the old ways. He's daring to marry beneath his status in society, and Philippe will not hear of it. To keep the way things have always been, he reverts to control tactics as he screams at his brother, *"I SHALL know how to prevent you!"* He is tenaciously clinging to the class in which he was birthed unwilling to accept change.

No doubt Philippe de Chagny was a complex man struggling with a changing world both politically and socially. I often wonder about his life prior to becoming the head of the family. He was thirty-two when his father passed way. Why hasn't he married? Why has he no children of his own? At that age, you would think he would have accomplished those two tasks in life, but he had not. We are given no explanation as to why.

Philippe, I believe, struggles with a changing world that grates against his ingrained beliefs. He clings to the way of life he knows, resists change, and desperately attempts to control his brother who wants to break away from the mold.

Philippe, unfortunately, fought change and attempted in vain to stop his brother from running away with Christine Daaé. His careless pursuit to stop him results in his own death. His body is discovered on the bank of the Opera lake. A sad ending indeed for a man with an excellent heart and an irreproachable conscience, who lost a battle with change.

As we all know, change is an inevitable part of life and most of us resist it on the spot rather than embracing its arrival. We tenaciously cling to what we have always known. We don't want our apple carts upset, or life to be different when we are comfortable.

It will knock on your door one day if it hasn't already. The question is, will you fight or embrace change? I like to think of Raoul and Christine as two that embraced change, for they left and built a new life together. Unfortunately, Philippe resisted change, and the result was his demise.

>(Posted Sunday, May 24, 2009)

Piagni

"A friend is one who knows you and loves you just the same."
Elbert Hubbard

In September 2009, I attended the Phantom Fans Week in Las Vegas at the Venetian Hotel, and I had the opportunity to meet the actor who plays Piangi in the production. He is a friendly, warm, and cheerful individual, and his presence made me pay particular attention to his interaction on stage with the other characters. As a result, I saw Piangi in an entirely new light as a character who exudes comedy and loyal support, but unfortunately experiences a tragic end.

Piangi is not in Leroux's original work. So who is this fellow? What does he portray and what lessons can we learn from his short, but important participation in the story itself?

First, it's quite obvious he is part of the comic relief in the opening scenes of Hannibal as he attempts to crawl on top of that elephant. We learned during the costume session in Vegas his cape weighs seventy pounds, so it is no wonder the guy has trouble!

Later in the scene, we see him standing by Carlotta watching her sing, comforting her after the accident occurs. He eventually storms off the stage with her, telling everyone they are a bunch of "*amateurs.*" In every performance I have attended, the audience laughs, and I am sure you have too.

What struck me while watching Piangi's interaction during the song Prima Donna, was the few words he spoke to the managers regarding Carlotta and how they do not deserve her. What a friend!

Let's face it, at this point, poor Carlotta is struggling to maintain her position as a lead soprano, feeling a tad bit slighted over Christine's stellar performance. She thinks she's no longer needed. Though the managers assure her she is valuable and want her to stay, you really doubt their sincerity.

Nevertheless, there stands faithful Piangi by her side as a friend and lover, watching over the woman he cares about and supporting her in any way he possibly can. Of course, at the "Point of No Return," we know he meets an untimely death at the hand of the Phantom.

What lesson can we learn? I think all of us need a Piangi in our lives. They are the friends that stand by us through thick and thin, support us when others dislike us, and encourage us when things are going rough. If you've ever had a Piangi-type friend in your life and lost them, you know how devastating that can be.

Why has it taken me so long to see Piangi's value in this story is beyond me. I can only say, bravo, to Ulbaldo Piangi for being the prime example of a faithful friend.

From the Phantom of the Opera

(Posted Thursday, September 24, 2009)

Note: In the new North American production, Piangi no longer climbs on an elephant at the end of the song but steps into a chariot and raises his knife.

Raoul de Chagny

"The first time that Raoul saw Christine at the Opera, he was charmed by the girl's beauty and by the sweet images of the past which it evoked..."
Gaston Leroux

Raoul, Vicomte de Chagny, is the representation of light and salvation, but is he saint or sinner? Well, that depends on your point of view.

Raoul, Vicomte de Chagny, is the representation of light and salvation, but is he saint or sinner? Well, that depends on your point of view.

In the movie version, Raoul's portrayal is one of a saint from the very beginning. He arrives at the opera house in his carriage pulled by white horses while we hear the rehearsal of Hannibal singing the words "savior" and "salvation" simultaneously as he enters through the stables. He is the "patron" of the opera house as if he is the "patron saint," a guardian who has arrived to save everyone from darkness. He is the supporter and benefactor of the Opera Populaire.

The lyrics Raoul sings in "All I Ask of You" overflow with Biblical references further identifying his saintly role:

He admonishes Christine not to speak of darkness. "*He brought them out of darkness*" *(Psalm 107:14)*

He tells her not to fear. *"Do not tremble, do not be afraid" (Isaiah 44:8)*

Raoul reassures her she is safe with him. *"No harm will befall you" (Psalm 91:10)*

He wants to be her freedom. *"Where the Spirit of the Lord is, there is freedom" (II Corinthians 3:17)*

He wants daylight to dry her tears. *"Will wipe away the tears from all faces" (Isaiah 25:8)*

He is with her always. *"Never will I leave you; never will I forsake you." (Hebrews 13:5)*

He will guard her. *"He guards the lives of his faithful ones and delivers them from the hand of the wicked." (Psalm 97:10)*

He will guide her. *"I will counsel you" (Psalm 32:8)*

He will be her shelter. "*He will hide me in the shelter*" *(Psalm 27:5)*

He will be her light. *"My light and my salvation" (Psalm 27:1)*

She is safe with him. *"You will keep us safe and protect us" (Psalm 12:7)*

Raoul represents all that is light, in contrast to the Phantom, who represents all that is darkness. Even during battles in the movie version in the cemetery and the lair, Raoul wears a cross under his white shirt, a sign of salvation and protection from the evil one. He rides a white horse as he speeds off to save Christine from the Phantom's deception at her father's grave. He does everything in his power to save Christine, even to the point of laying down his life to free her from the Phantom. Raoul is a saint.

How do others view him? Christine loves Raoul because he can protect her and give her a better life. She looks to him as a father figure. In Leroux's version, however, she judges him for his lack of compassion towards the Phantom.

"Raoul, why do you condemn a man whom you have never seen, whom no one knows and about whom you yourself know nothing?"

Raoul has fallen in love with his childhood sweetheart. The Phantom declares he was bound to love her, once he heard her sing. Leroux writes the depth of his love:

"Raoul suffered, for she was very beautiful and he was shy and dared not confess his love, even to himself. And then came the lightning flash of the gala performance: the heavens torn asunder and an angel's voice heard upon earth for the delight of mankind and the utter capture of his heart."

Raoul de Chagny was head over heels in love with Christine Daaé.

How does the Phantom view him? No doubt, he sees him as a rival, of course, and a threat to his influence over the opera house and to his desire for Christine.

What are his sins? He embodies the light of day that never shows him compassion. He represents the world of society that has rejected him. He calls Raoul an insolent boy, negating his manhood. He is foolishly brave, invading his territory and daring to share in his triumph. He rants that he is a slave of fashion, indicating his shallowness. The unseen genius calls him an ignorant fool. Raoul is the world that shows the Phantom no compassion.

How does Raoul view the Phantom? A rival, of course. At first, he denies his existence to Christine in an attempt to discredit him. He views him as a threat, which he must stop and destroy. He gives him no credit for being a genius who inspired Christine's voice, only saying he is a genius gone mad. He is unable to relate to the Phantom's plight of ugliness and isolation. He repeatedly states in Leroux's version that he hates Erik. The Phantom is a dangerous rival for Christine's affections because he can touch her soul in places that Raoul is incapable of reaching.

How interesting that both of these men are jealous of each other. The Phantom is jealous of Raoul because he can provide Christine the things in life he cannot: beauty, acceptance, wealth, and status. Raoul is jealous of the Phantom because he can provide Christine things in life he cannot: inspiration, music, and passion. Raoul touches her purity. The Phantom touches her passion. Neither possesses her heart completely. Each possesses only that part they are able to reach.

Raoul and the Phantom are symbols of the age-old struggle of light versus darkness, jealous of what each possesses. Not many of us live blissful, prosperous lives full of beauty. Perhaps that is another reason we relate more to Erik, for he embodies all that we long for and the pain we sometimes feel.

What are your thoughts? What do you see in Raoul? Is he a saint or sinner? Do you envy or pity him? As you ponder the thoughts, look deeply inside. Do you struggle with jealousy over what another possesses in life that you do not? I am sure that answer depends on your point of view behind the mask of your life.

Perhaps another lesson we can learn from Raoul's character, is whether we are saint or sinner, we are all in need of redemption from our negative qualities.

(POSTED SATURDAY, MARCH 22, 2008)

The Phantom

"Yes, he existed in flesh and blood, although he assumed the complete appearance of a real phantom. . . "
Gaston Leroux

We have studied Erik (his humanity) and the Opera Ghost (his persona), but not the Phantom of the Opera. Ooh, sounds mysterious! That is preciously the point.

I find it quite interesting after searching my PDF version of Gaston Leroux's book sitting on my computer desktop, that Leroux only uses the term Phantom twice in the entire work. Once in the title and once in the introduction, as follows:

"Yes, he existed in flesh and blood, although he assumed the complete appearance of a real phantom; that is to say, of a spectral shade."

In the remainder of the book, the Phantom is referred to as either the Opera Ghost or Erik. Leroux insists he existed in flesh and blood but assumed the appearance of a phantom—a spectral shade, which is a ghost with a shadow-like appearance. Pull out the dictionary and you will find phantom refers to something with no substantial existence. So is he or is he not? Is he real or a ghost? Is he man or phantom? Perhaps as Erik lurks around the opera house, he wants to leave that question with you.

In the play and movie, a few characters, but not all, use the term Phantom of the Opera. Meg, Christine, and Raoul call him the Phantom. Of course, Meg and Christine possess an upfront personal knowledge he exists and they are good at screaming, *"It's the Phantom of the Opera!"* Our dear, Raoul, however, says he is a fable and does not exist. Later, of course, he changes his mind with the noose around his neck. Years later in the dilapidated opera house during the sale, the auctioneer references the famous disaster and the strange affair of the Phantom.

Erik calls himself the Phantom.

So why did Leroux choose the name *The Phantom of the Opera*? Why didn't he name the book the "Illusive Opera Ghost" or "Erik the Madman in the Opera Cellars"? I think it is a rational question to ask. Is Leroux teasing us with the same question since he keeps telling us Erik really existed, but in the next breath refers to him as a spectral shade, apparent to the senses, but does not exist? Somebody make up his or her mind!

Erik in his humanity is the man we examined behind the mask that touches the core of our hearts with his inward pain. The Opera Ghost, his persona, is the projection he gives to the world when he allows you to see him, reminding you he is walking death on the outside. Finally, behind the scenes, lurking in the shadows, out of public view, he takes on the appearance of a phantom, the ultimate cover or disguise making you question whether he is real. All this strange speculation about his existence gives birth to the mysterious fables about the Phantom of the Opera.

Surely, everyone occasionally plays the role of a phantom. Haven't you heard the phrase, "Is that guy for real?"

(POSTED WEDNESDAY, JUNE 25, 2008)

Section Two
Emotions in the Phantom of the Opera

Anger
Anguish
Confusion
Despair
Doubt
Fear
Hate
Jealousy
Loss
Love
Memories
Obsession
Passion
Seduction

Anger

*"I should always hear the superhuman
cry of grief and rage which he uttered when the terrible sight
appeared before my eyes."*
Gaston Leroux

Wait a minute. Did we hear the Phantom right? Did he just say, *"Damn you! Curse you!"* I thought he loved Christine. Now he's damning and cursing her and calling her names? What's up with that?

Prying Pandora! Pandora was the first woman created by the Greek gods endowed with unique gifts. She opened a jar out of curiosity and released all sorts of evils upon humanity. (Not much different from Eve biting that apple.) Did he equate Christine's act as prying curiosity, which released his evil reaction when she stripped off his mask?

Demon! Quite self-explanatory, an evil spirit, malicious and wicked. He calls his beloved Christine a demon but equates himself as one inwardly. Psychologists call this behavior projection, which is a defense mechanism we use to project our own unacceptable thoughts or emotions upon another.

Lying Delilah! Delilah is the woman who betrayed Samson in the Biblical story. Samson was the strongest man in the entire world, and his enemies the Philistines wanted to destroy him. He loved a Philistine woman, Delilah, who covertly attempted to find the secret to his strength, and then betrayed him to his enemies. Christine is trying to find the secret behind the mask, but he's accusing her of lying about her sincerity and betraying him. A prophetic statement, I think.

Viper! Now he's referencing her as a poisonous snake lying in the grass ready to strike with venom.

So what triggered this outbreak of rage and anger against the woman he loved? Christine, as we would say in modern times, "pushed his buttons," "triggered a reaction," or "hit a sore spot," however you would like to term the act. Her removal of his mask exposed the most painful part of who he was as a human being—his physical deformity. Unfortunately, she did not only do it once, she did it twice! Each time elicited the same reaction of rage.

Erik's reaction in the book is violent. He hisses at her, curses her, and pulls her by the hair. In the play he curses and cries, and crawls across the stage in grief. *(See Note Below)* In the movie, he acts violently shoving Christine down, physically and verbally abusing the woman he supposedly loves.

I think all of us possess trigger points. Painful reminders of our lives that are sore spots in places we wish not to be touched. Like jabbing at an open wound, we cry and react in unbelievable pain. We yell at those we love and hurt those close to us.

The scene in the book, play, and the movie is another example of Erik's humanity. You may have pulled the symbolic mask off another person out of curiosity and been the brunt of someone's outburst. Perhaps you had your own mask removed and lashed out at the one who exposed and poked you.

We all have those places of pain we do not wish touched by others. Through the story, we know Erik's pain, understand how he feels, and forgive his rash behavior. It is definitely one of those "been there - done that" moments to which we all relate.

At the end of the scene, Christine sheds tears and hands to Erik his mask, the dignity she stripped from him, no doubt sorrowful she caused him such pain out of idle curiosity. He places it back on his face and rises. I have often pondered her act exposing him a second time, especially knowing the great pain it would cause and the response it would elicit.

The question remains for you, what's your trigger point? What sore spot in your life sets you off when touched? We all have them. I know I do, so please don't strip off my mask.

(POSTED THURSDAY, OCTOBER 30, 2008)

NOTE: THIS CHOREOGRAPHED MOVEMENT IN THE STAGE VERSION OF *THE PHANTOM OF THE OPERA* HAS BEEN REMOVED IN THE NORTH AMERICAN TOUR. THE PHANTOM NO LONGER CRAWLS TO CHRISTINE ACROSS THE STAGE BUT INSTEAD REMAINS STANDING.

Anguish

"He had let go of me at last and was dragging himself about on the floor, uttering terrible sobs." Gaston Leroux

Lately I've been focusing on a different authorship and was pondering Erik's anguish. I remembered words written by Leroux, which shook me once again and shed light upon Erik's pain that I've never pondered before. Both of these quotes of Christine come from the scene of Erik's unmasking in front of her and painfully speak of the anguish of his soul. It is Erik's suffering.

"*Yes, if I lived to be a hundred, I should always hear the superhuman cry of grief and rage which he uttered when the terrible sight appeared before my eyes...*"

I happened to pick up the Bible this week, which I rarely do, and oddly was drawn to the Book of Job. It's not an uplifting book to read. It focuses on one man who loses everything—family, possessions, and health and enters into an extremely painful season in his life. It's a book of anguish and suffering penned thousands of years ago. As I read passages, they flew off the page as the voice of Erik expressing his anguish in my ears.

Consider the following quotes cursing his existence:

". . . opened his mouth and cursed the day of his birth. Let the day perish on which I was to be born, and the night which said, a boy is conceived. May that day be darkness; Let not God above care for it, nor light shine on it." (Job 3:1-4)

"I loathe my very life; therefore I will give free rein to my complaint and speak out in the bitterness of my soul." (Job 10:1)

Consider his questions why:

"Why did I not perish at birth, and die as I came from the womb?" (Job 3:11)

"Why then did you bring me out of the womb? I wish I had died before any eye saw me. If only I had never come into being, or had been carried straight from the womb to the grave!" (Job 10:18-19)

"Why is light given to those in misery, and life to the bitter of soul, to those who long for death that does not come, who search for it more than for hidden treasure, who are filled with gladness and rejoice when they reach the grave?" (Job 3:20-22)

Human suffering is not a topic we care to focus upon, but when we look at Erik, he is truly a picture of human suffering and anguish. His extreme pain is evident in his actions and heard in the cry of his sobs.

We all experience various forms of suffering and anguish in our lives. It is true; some experience more than others do. Throughout the ages, humans have called it by many names: your cross to bear, your lot in life, fate dealing you a rotten hand, bad karma, etc. Whatever term you give it, whether you are religious or a non-believer, anguish, and suffering is as universal as the air we breathe.

Although we can empathize with those who suffer, we cannot bear the anguish or pains of another. I cannot imagine the totality of Erik's anguished soul or the deep effect it had on his psyche. Like you, I can only read about it, see it portrayed on stage and film, and ponder what he must have felt. His anguish is his own. "*Each heart knows its own bitterness . . .*" (Proverbs 14:10)

Unfortunately, we are not given reasons for our anguish and pain. We often ask why. I know I'm not the only one to lift my head to the heavens and question, in fact, demand a reason for my own personal sufferings. No doubt, we have all heard the same silence. We can only speculate, or like Job's friends, be judged by others for why we suffer.

We could ask the same questions about Erik. Why was he burdened with such a horrid deformity and relegated to a life of suffering and rejection? On the other hand, we could also ask why he was blessed with such marvelous musical genius in return.

It's here at this point of anguish we all relate in some way. As a result, we are profoundly drawn to *The Phantom of the Opera*, which grips our hearts and will not let go.

(POSTED WEDNESDAY, AUGUST 26, 2009)

Confusion

*"I have a letter of Christine's . . . relating to this period,
which suggests a feeling of absolute dismay."*
Gaston Leroux

Twisted in every way is an interesting statement that Christine makes in the midst of a difficult time in her life where she must make a life-changing decision. I believe it's something we all go through at one time or another; that is, being faced with a very difficult decision knowing it will carry with it consequences.

Let's look at Christine's time with Raoul as she cries on his shoulder bearing her heart and pleading with him not to make her go through with the Phantom's Opera. Why is Christine struggling? She is struggling with a choice. To find freedom, she will pay a price.

Christine is at a difficult crossroad. She must betray the man who birthed her voice. She feels a great sense of gratitude to Erik for what he has done for her, but she wants her freedom. She struggles to break from the shackles of Erik's influence so she can pursue a life with Raoul. What's the poor girl suppose to do? Eventually, she makes a decision, but it carries consequences. To obtain her freedom, she must hurt the Phantom in the process, and she fears horrors await for her as a result.

She follows her heart, and her fears happen. The one she chooses to leave, instead of willingly letting her go, forces her to stay with him. The irony of the story closely relates to the story of Little Lotte, who kept the caged bird that died unfulfilled. The Phantom eventually realizes that keeping Christine captive would do the same to her. Now he learns what true love is all about. It's no longer obsession keeping her by force. Instead, he allows her to go free and live the life she really desires with Raoul.

Similar situations happen to us in real life. We are faced with difficult decisions and need to leave, but feel we owe that person something. Choosing to stay would no doubt make us unhappy. Being forced to stay would make us bitter. Leaving anyway and experiencing the consequences from the unhappy receiver of our decision sometimes hurts.

The greatest gift we can give anyone, however, is the freedom to leave and the gift of flight, even if it costs us in the process. Not every relationship is necessarily meant for eternity. Some relationships are only here for a season, and it takes wisdom to discern between the two. Did it cost Erik to let go of Christine? Of course, it did. Did Christine appreciate Erik allowing her to leave? What do you think?

What lesson can we learn through her confusion? First, have the courage to make the decisions that are right for you, even if you must pay a price. It is possible others will be disappointed or hurt by your decisions, but do not let that hinder you from following the path you know is right for your life.

Second, if there is someone in your life that wants to fly, open the door to the cage, and let them go. Everyone should be entitled to follow their dreams, especially when it is in our hands to give them the gift of freedom and a little push along the way. Letting go is more freeing than hanging on to something that is not yours to keep.

(POSTED TUESDAY, DECEMBER 9, 2008)

Doubt

"He no longer doubted the almost supernatural powers of the Angel of Music."
Gaston Leroux

Not long ago, I rented a movie entitled *Doubt*, starring Meryl Streep and Philip Seymour Hoffman. The movie contains a powerful message and an ending that I frankly found haunting. The theme, of course, is doubt and the power it possesses.

Leroux skillfully employs doubt throughout *The Phantom of the Opera*. He uses it in various forms. His characters express their uncertainty, distrust, and skepticism over certain matters, and he speaks of his own doubts as well. Let's look at a few instances.

Raoul is one character riddled with doubt over Christine. He doubts her love, the truth of her statements, and even her virtuous conduct as a woman. The most glaring doubt he harbors is whether she truly loves him. It's obvious, her words say one thing, but her actions display another. As a result, Raoul expresses his doubts.

"I doubted your love for me, during those hours."

Though Christine tries to assure him that his doubts are unfounded because she acted out of fright with regard to Erik, Raoul continues to question her sincerity.

"*You are frightened... but do you love me? If Erik were good-looking, would you love me, Christine?*"

Of course, then comes the infamous kiss between Christine and Raoul on the rooftop as she attempts to convince him of her love. Was Raoul convinced or did he still harbor his doubts?

Christine harbored her own doubts about Raoul's ability to free her from Erik's influence. As they ascended to the rooftop, Leroux says she entertained the possibility and allowed herself this doubt. What doubt? Apparently, she was convinced that no one could save her from Erik's power. For one brief moment, she allowed herself to believe that there could be freedom, rather than to doubt.

"*She allowed herself this doubt, which was an encouragement...*"

Philippe, as we all know, vehemently opposed the union between Raoul and Christine. Did he have doubts that Raoul was totally crazy for loving Christine? Apparently, but when he attempts to run away and elope with her, Philippe's doubts are dispelled and he truly thinks his brother is mad!

"*And the count, who no longer entertained any doubt of his brother's madness, in his turn darted into that infernal underground maze.*"

Of course, the most doubt expressed in the story swirls around the Opera Ghost, our dear Erik. A few of our characters have their doubts about Erik. It takes Christine's disappearance for Raoul to no longer doubt Erik's power:

"Raoul's first thought, after Christine Daaé's fantastic disappearance, was to accuse Erik. He no longer doubted the almost supernatural powers of the Angel of Music, in this domain of the Opera in which he had set up his empire."

The managers at first doubted the antics of the Ghost, until they were finally convinced of his powers as well.

"Richard and Moncharmin turned pale. There was no longer any doubt about the witchcraft. 'The ghost!' muttered Moncharmin."

The Persian often doubted Erik's words. Regarding the fate of Christine and Raoul, it took tears to convince him otherwise:

"The Persian asked him no questions. He was quite reassured as to the fate of Raoul Chagny and Christine Daaé; no one could have doubted the word of the weeping Erik that night."

Our author is definitely the weaver of doubt, but the biggest one he toys with throughout the entire story is whether Erik truly lived! He tells of his investigations into the fable, his discussions with the Persian, his discovery of the famous bundle of letters written by Christine. Then he makes the statement that he no longer has doubt the Ghost truly existed and penned the following:

"I was at first inclined to be suspicious; but when the Persian had told me, with child-like candor, all that he knew about the ghost and had handed me the proofs of the ghost's existence—including the strange correspondence of Christine Daaé—to do as I pleased with, I was no longer able

to doubt. No, the ghost was not a myth!"

Of course, that is the one big question that surrounds this story. Is it truly an investigation by Gaston Leroux into the existence of the Ghost? Is the prologue and epilogue truth, and the middle merely his fanciful fiction rendition of the events as they transpired. Dare I say that the entire thing is a fabrication and the result of his wild imagination as he writes the novel?

As I look at the book sitting up on my desk next to my computer, the pages appear wrapped in an aura of mystery. As stated in the play, perhaps it is a strange affair that will never fully be explained. Will any of us ever know if it was a carefully crafted story of illusion to make you think it was real? Did Erik truly live or is he just the figment of Leroux's imagination? As I stated before, Leroux lived in an era when the art of illusion was big business. Was this just another illusion as a means of entertainment?

Do my questions create doubt in your heart? What evidence do you have there is an ounce of truth in the story? Do you believe or do you doubt that Erik, the Phantom of the Opera, truly existed? Perhaps Leroux was just weaving a tale after all. Oh, excuse me; I'm sowing seeds of doubt. One small planting, a little watering, doubt will grow, and the truth will become shades of gray.

Doubt—a five-letter word packed with power.

(POSTED SATURDAY, AUGUST 8, 2009)

Fear

"I think that I shall not be far from the truth if I ascribe her action simply to fear . . . Christine Daaé was frightened by what had happened to her."
Gaston Leroux

Another emotion that plays strongly in the book and subsequent works is the element of fear. *The Phantom of the Opera* reads like a classic horror story, and Leroux is good at producing trepidation. Fear touches nearly every character involved with Erik.

Meg Giry loved to tease the young ballerinas until their blood ran cold. One scene in the book tells of all the ballet brats crowding around her waiting to hear horror stories about the Ghost.

"They were there, side by side, leaning forward simultaneously in one movement of entreaty and fear, communicating their terror to one another, taking a keen pleasure in feeling their blood freeze in their veins."

The Managers feared the Ghost. They whispered when they spoke fearing OG would overhear. When Joseph Buquet was found dead, it served as a brutal reminder of the consequences of dismissing the Ghost's wishes.

The Persian feared Erik. He knew his

capabilities to kill, trap, torture, and he called him a monster. Leroux states the Persian feared for the safety of others who encountered the Opera Ghost. He feared crossing the lake to the lair.

"*I fear that more than one of those men—old scene-shifters, old door-shutters—who have never been seen again were simply tempted to cross the lake...*"

Raoul dealt keenly with fear. He feared for Christine's safety, and he feared death at the hand of Erik. When he and the Persian are in the mirrored torture chamber facing death, the Persian recounts for them both:

"*M. de Chagny and I began to yell like madmen. Fear spurred us on.*"

In the play and movie, poor Raoul hangs with a noose around his neck about ready to experience death. Do you think he was afraid?

Christine feared for Raoul's life. She feared Erik though, at one point, she denies it to Raoul. However, later she tells Raoul of her fear of returning underground once again to Erik's lair. She tells Erik that he frightens her. Leroux writes her actions were motivated by fear.

"*I think that I shall not be far from the truth if I ascribe her action simply to fear. Yes, I believe that Christine Daaé was frightened by what had happened to her.*"

Raoul thought Christine's fear of Erik in Leroux's version was really a bad-boy attraction, which I find quite interesting.

"*Why, you love him! Your fear, your terror, all of that is just love and love of the most exquisite kind, the kind which people do not admit even to themselves," said Raoul bitterly. "The kind that gives you a thrill, when you think of it. Picture it: a man who lives in a palace underground!"*

Erik recognizes the fear in Christine and tells her not to fear. When he sees her cry, he exclaims:

"*You are crying! You are afraid of me!*"

Did Erik have fears? Christine speaks to him and begs him to show his face:

"*Show me your face without fear!*"

Though Erik is the focus of everyone's fear, he struggles with one major fear; that is, the fear of removing his mask and exposing his deformity. Surely, if you dig deeper into his personality, you will find many other fears lurking beneath the surface.

The story has been portrayed in many ways from horror to romance. It has the element of fear woven throughout, and all the characters are afraid of Erik in one way or the other. One underlying theme, however, is that fear comes in many forms. Christine feared Erik and a life of captivity. Raoul feared torture and death at the hands of Erik. The Persian feared the monstrous capabilities Erik possessed. The ballet corps feared Meg's next horror story. The managers feared the Opera Ghost's wrath.

Do you see the story as a classic horror story or a romance? For some reason, I already think I know the answer to that question from the majority of fans who love *The Phantom of the Opera*. However, I encourage honesty in your reflection. Imagine yourself as Christine dragged down to the lair by an apparent lunatic. Would you be afraid or attracted to Erik? I suppose it depends on how much you like that bad-boy attraction!

(POSTED SUNDAY, MARCH 15, 2009)

Hate

"'Oh, I hate him!' cried Raoul."
Gaston Leroux

If you are wondering how I pull all these tidbits out of the story, it's simple. Gaston Leroux's novel is public domain. You can search the Internet and find PDF forms of the book free. Once you download and save it to your computer, you have the ability to search text. I really encourage you to read the book. As wonderful as the play and movie are, they really do not do the characters justice. Reading the original work provides you the opportunity to search out the depths of each character.

Hate is another emotion often referenced in Leroux's work, which motivates some of our characters throughout the story. Frankly, I cannot write about the meaning of love, without exploring the opposite of the spectrum, which is hate. Whenever we hate something or someone, it encompasses strong emotions of revulsion and disgust. In today's vernacular, it just means we can't stand something or someone. Have you ever hated anything or anyone?

Let's look at some of the characters and the

hatred they experience in the story. Of course, all of the references below come from Leroux's version to help shed light on everyone's motivation.

Raoul's hatred of Erik is the most pronounced. At least Leroux clearly states that he struggles with hating Erik, and at times is so mad at Christine, he expresses disgust toward her that she does not share the same feelings. The first instance where Leroux mentions Raoul's hatred of Erik is outside Christine's dressing room door after her gala performance. He listens and hears Erik's voice inside, and Leroux pens his hateful response.

"*At one and the same time, he had learned what love meant, and hatred. He knew that he loved. He wanted to know whom he hated.*"

Raoul discovers he has a rival for Christine's affections. Our mild-mannered Raoul is struggling with emotion that he apparently has never experienced with such intensity—hate.

Later in the story, Raoul confronts Christine wanting to know if she hates Erik as well.

"*And you, Christine, tell me, do you hate him too?*"

Christine says she does not, and then he demands to know what feelings Erik inspires in her if she does not hate him. Of course, he assumes her feelings are those of love. Raoul, filled with what Leroux terms as "*childish hatred*," sneers at her in a despicable manner. You cannot really blame the man. After all, he worships the ground she walks on. Hatred is a response toward those who betray our hearts.

What about Erik? Does he have a heart filled

with hatred? Christine tells of a time when she sings a duet with Erik, and she describes the feelings he pours forth during the song.

"As for him, his voice thundered forth his revengeful soul at every note. Love, jealousy, hatred, burst out around us in harrowing cries."

There is no doubt Erik hated Raoul and what he represented, as well as the world that showed him no compassion.

On the other hand, Christine does not say that she hates Erik. She confesses to Raoul, *"He fills me with horror, and I do not hate him."* Apparently, the love he has for her prevents her from hating him in return.

"How can I hate him, Raoul? Think of Erik at my feet, in the house on the lake, underground. He accuses himself, he curses himself, he implores my forgiveness! He confesses his cheat. He loves me! He lays at my feet an immense and tragic love. He has carried me off for love! He has imprisoned me with him, underground, for love. But he respects me: he crawls, he moans, he weeps!"

As the story continues, it seems as if Raoul is the only one harboring hate in his heart for Erik. He inquires if the Persian feels as he does.

"You must certainly hate Erik!"

However, to his dismay, the Persian replies:

"No, sir. I do not hate him. If I hated, he would long ago have ceased doing harm."

The Persian confesses that he has forgiven Erik for any harm he received at his hand.

What is the antidote for hate? The wise Persian gives us what we all need to hear, *"I have forgiven him the harm which he has done me."* Truly, that is the only cure for hatred—a good dose of forgiveness. Hatred, like jealousy, is another destructive emotion that have the tendency to destroy us from the inside out. We think that our hatred hurts the other person, but in reality, it only hurts us inside. Forgiveness, of course, is the balm.

Do some people deserve our forgiveness for their actions? Probably not. However, the story of *The Phantom of the Opera* is a story of redemption and a cry for love, not revenge. For one to find redemption, one must first find forgiveness.

If you harbor hatred in your heart, take a lesson from the story and forgive. It will do your heart good.

(POSTED SATURDAY, MARCH 21, 2009)

Jealousy

*"Raoul's fingers clutched at his flesh,
above his jealous heart."*
Gaston Leroux

Jealousy has been on my mind lately. It's another emotion in *The Phantom of the Opera*, which I like to call our psychological playground. You may not be struggling with jealousy presently, but it does occasionally knock at our door wearing different masks. Do you see any jealousy lurking around the opera house?

Before you cringe and think that I am about to preach, relax. It's just a quote. However, the Bible can be a hot book. There are quite a few seductive love stories hidden inside. One verse in the book of Song of Solomon has a very poignant statement about jealousy. For those of you who don't know, it's a book about love and sex. King Solomon is the author, and he happened to have seven hundred wives and three hundred concubines. He must have possessed some first-hand knowledge on the subject to write the following:

"For love is as strong as death, its jealousy unyielding as the grave. It burns like blazing fire, like a mighty flame." (Song of Solomon 8:6)

Jealousy is a strong emotion. It drives men to kill, war, steal and fight, just to name a few. Jealousy, as I think about it in the context of romantic love, is resentment against a rival for another's affection. Certainly that was the case between the Phantom and Raoul. Both were in the love with the same woman. Both were rivals for her affection, and both possessed qualities the other did not have, which drew Christine to each of them in different ways.

I do not doubt that Erik felt intense jealousy toward Raoul, his rival, for Christine's affection. Raoul represented all that Erik did not possess, such as beauty, wealth, and title. The Phantom could offer none of these things to Christine. Yet oddly enough, the Phantom possessed qualities that Raoul lacked such as musical genius and passion. During the scene of the "Point of No Return," there was no doubt jealousy that consumed Raoul as he witnessed the obvious passionate attraction between the Phantom and Christine. In fact, he's moved to tears in the movie.

Jealousy is a consuming emotion that burns like a mighty flame. Unfortunately, the possessor of jealousy usually ends up consumed by the very emotion they embrace. Jealousy is unyielding, hard to appease, and cruel as the grave. The emotion is draining and useless. It takes a mature individual to realize the emotion carries a hefty price tag. Our dear Phantom allowed jealousy to consume him. In his attempt to possess Christine, he ultimately pays a price.

I think everyone is touched with jealousy sometime in his or her life. Perhaps not the overwhelming jealousy surrounding romantic love, but the subtle jealousy of envy and resentment towards what others possess, whether or not we deem them our rival.

It is probably best when jealousy comes knocking at your door that you just take a quick glance to see who is there, check the price tag, and say you are not interested. Better to turn away the cruel emotion rather than to embrace it and die in its flames.

(POSTED SUNDAY, JUNE 29, 2008)

Loss

"They kissed like a despairing brother and sister who have been smitten with a common loss and who meet to mourn a dead parent."
Gaston Leroux

Another aspect of human pain I see within *The Phantom of the Opera* is that of loss. We can lose things, relationships, and loved ones. Each instance of loss carries disappointment, but some instances of loss carry great pain and suffering. Loss affects our lives deeply. It steals our joy, ruins our hope, and brings despondency to our hearts. In dealing with the pain, we can lose part of ourselves in the process as well.

What losses do you see woven into the story of *The Phantom of the Opera*? Leroux speaks of Christine's loss of her father and that it stole the song from her heart.

"She seemed to have lost with him, her voice, her soul, and her genius."

It changed the way she looked at life:

". . . she acquired a distaste for everything in life, including her art."

Raoul lost his mother at birth and his father

twelve years later. Then, of course, Erik lost Christine to Raoul. The tale is filled with instances of loss.

Loss is simply something we once possessed that is no longer ours. We can lose things that may be important to us, but things are replaceable simply by buying another. We can lose relationships, but relationships are replaceable usually as others come across our path and into our lives to fill the void. However, losses in our lives that are irreplaceable hurt the deepest. In those losses, we have the potential of losing part of ourselves in the process of dealing with the pain.

What helps us through a loss? Often it takes others intervening in our lives during the process of grieving. In the instance of Christine, the Angel of Music returned to her the desire to sing. Through a series of personal heartaches, I lost the desire to write for many years until friends flamed the smoldering ashes and pushed me to pick up a pen. I truly believe that in the hour of our greatest losses, our greatest achievements are born.

Though we all experience loss in our lives, we can gain things in the process of restoration, such as comfort and new friends. In our own loss, we also have opportunities to give back to others who experience the same loss we have. We learn to weep with those who weep, and ultimately comfort others with the same comfort given to us.

(POSTED SATURDAY, JUNE 7, 2008)

Love

"He loves me! He lays at my feet an immense and tragic love. He has carried me off for love! He has imprisoned me with him, underground, for love!"
Gaston Leroux

After pondering the next emotion to dissect, love is tugging at my heart. For *The Phantom of the Opera*, I want to focus on the types of love found in the story. However, to understand what love is, you must understand its meaning.

The word for love in the original Greek language refers to three types of emotions. In the English language, we see a four-letter word that we think is all encompassing in the definition, but the English word for love narrowly defines its meaning and does not do it justice.

The Greek language uses three words to define love:

Eros - love that is sensual and passionate in nature.

Agape - love we associate with people such as our spouses, children, parents. *Agape* is also the Greek description of God's love.

Philia - platonic and loyal love we give to

friends, family, and community.

In *The Phantom of the Opera*, we see all three types of love displayed. There is the passionate, sensual love filled with desire and longing the Phantom has for Christine—*Eros*. We witness the caring and loving affection of Raoul for Christine, who portrays salvation and light—*Agape*. Madame Giry portrays love as the friend—*Philia*.

We all possess different ideas regarding the concept of love, which is formed through our life experiences. The treatment we receive from others who declare they love us, paints a picture of truth or distortion. Erik, in his humanity, never received love from another human. Rejected and abandoned as a child naturally formed a distorted perception of love in his eyes.

Whether it's the love of a friend, sibling, parent or mate, we crave affection. Why? I believe it's because love nourishes our soul and keeps us whole. Your body cannot live without food and water as nourishment, and your soul cannot live without love in some form. We use the term "love-starved" and rightly so. Without it, we shrivel up to nothing but skin and bones emotionally, as Erik did alone in isolation. Erik's cry echoes in my heart every day:

"All I wanted was to be loved for myself."

Why do we crave love so desperately but find it so difficult to give consistently in return? Is it a sign of the times? Here's a thought. If the Phantom lived in the twenty-first century, would we give him the love and acceptance or would we take him to the nearest plastic surgeon instead?

Here I go, poking at you once again in love! Just to clarify; that's *Philia* love.

(POSTED SUNDAY, JULY 13, 2008)

Memories

"Think of Me."
Song by Andrew Lloyd Webber

As I ponder what to write, I remember Christine's debut on stage as she prophetically sings, "Think of Me." If you carefully read and listen to the lyrics, they are pleas to remember fondly the good times, not dwell on unfulfilled desires and realize that life contains seasons rather than constants. When New Year arrives, it is good advice to apply to our own lives.

Change is an inevitable part of life we all experience in one form or another. Life is full of seasons; it evolves and changes. In relationships, people enter and leave us throughout our lifetime. Each time that occurs, we stand at the crossroads of saying goodbye to someone or something, and we face choices on how to handle the memories left behind. We can choose to think fondly of our past or dwell on the negatives.

Everyone in the story of *The Phantom of the Opera* faces the same choice on how to handle the evolution of the story. As we think of Erik and

Christine, there were no doubt memories of one another long after their parting. Christine's prophetic words in the song "Think of Me" is heartfelt. There would never be a day she will not think of him, and she hopes there is never a day he will not think of her with fondness. Their comfort in parting is to dwell on what they shared, rather than to mourn what they lost.

Midnight each year on January 1, a door opens and you walk into a New Year. Will you turn around and look behind you as you pass through the door? Will there be pain, regrets or bitterness you'll carry with you like baggage across the threshold? Will you resolve to forget what is behind and reach for what is ahead with anticipation and thankfulness? The best advice I can give my readers is to keep focused on what is ahead with hope in your heart. If memories of the former year come to mind, think fondly of your past, don't hold onto any bitterness, and remember life is filled with seasons.

(POSTED TUESDAY, DECEMBER 30, 2008)

Obsession

"All extremes of feeling are allied with madness."
Virginia Woolf

Obsession. What is it? It is a disturbing preoccupation with someone or something. Obsession crosses a dangerous line when desire becomes unreasonable and one loses touch with reality. At this stage, the obsessed person turns toward violence to obtain what they want. Was the Phantom obsessed with Christine or did he love her?

Christine had been in Erik's life for many years. Coming to live at the opera house as a child, Erik took an interest in her. He became her protector, an angel, a guide in her father's absence. He watched her grow from a young girl into womanhood. He spoke to her in the night and came to her in her dreams. Through the walls, through the mirrors, and in the shadows he was there.

He recognizes Christine's potential as a singer. He tutors and develops her skill. Erik gives her a voice, which expresses his musical genius. Christine's talent in many ways is the Phantom's creation. He wants and needs her to sing his music.

She is his glory, his triumphant, which he does not wish to share with another. Christine is Erik's entire focus in life and constantly on his mind.

As she matures into a beautiful sexual young woman, he begins to desire her, worship her, and fantasize about her. He plans her future as a singer and his wife. He fills the lair with her portrait, opera scenes of her singing, and a wax figure of her body in a wedding gown. He surrounds his life with reminders of Christine everywhere in his lair and dreams of the day she will belong to him alone.

What happened to Erik? Did he try to fill the void of his solitude with one thing alone? Did his obsessive thoughts turn around and consume him in return? When does one cross the line from reality into dangerous obsession?

The obsession became disturbing and unhealthy when it drove Erik to commit violent acts. Having never loved or been loved, Erik was immature and did not understand the meaning of love. He believed he loved Christine when he was actually obsessed.

Erik learns the meaning of true love when he releases Christine from captivity. In tears, when she returns the ring, he tells her, "*Christine, I love you.*" Erik now knows love. Obsession is no longer the driving force of his actions. True love is acted upon in his willingness to give her freedom.

Obsession does not sacrifice—it only takes. Love sacrifices—it only gives.

On my Phantom journey, I meet many individuals who say they are obsessed with *The Phantom of the Opera*. Though I do not believe it is an obsession in the literal unhealthy sense, I think we have a preoccupation because we relate to Erik. Every once in a while it's probably a healthy thing to shake ourselves back into reality and not live so vicariously through the story.

(POSTED SATURDAY, MARCH 1, 2008)

Passion

". . . what passions, what crimes had surrounded the idyll of Raoul and the sweet and charming Christine!"
Gaston Leroux

Do you remember Mr. Spock on Star Trek, the alien without emotions? Pretty sad living your life with only logic, never experiencing love, hate, jealousy, passion, lust, obsession, despair, joy, and fear. Emotions are powerful. They drive our thoughts and influence our behavior. Having a Mr. Spock-like personality in life would be boring. Where is the fun in that? Probably the only advantage would be you would never feel the pain of a broken heart.

I must confess when I was born, I was overly wired with emotion. I am definitely an extremist in this area. When I feel emotion, I feel emotion. I laugh outrageously. I cry uncontrollably. Maybe that is why I am obsessed with *The Phantom of the Opera*. I fall hard for things that deeply touch my heart.

Passion in *The Phantom of the Opera* is everywhere. It is powerfully portrayed in the play and movie among our three main characters: the Phantom, Christine, and Raoul. The hottest passion exists between Christine and Erik. Watch the "Point of No Return" and you need a fan to cool you down.

What is passion? It's a powerful and compelling emotion exhibited in both love and hate. Romantic passion is an emotion filled with strong love, mixed with sexual desire for another person. The Phantom felt passion and desire for Christine, even though he had never been with a woman. He was more than willing to experience his first lesson, as he sings to her the questions he desperately wants to be answered.

Christine is obviously drawn to the Phantom in a passionate way, more so than to Raoul. Probably a little bit of that bad-boy attraction is going on, and Raoul actually accuses her of such desires in the original work.

A few weeks ago, we had one of those water cooler moments at work with a few of the girls talking about *The Phantom of the Opera* and passion. Some of the women were married, some single, some divorced. I found it interesting that the majority never experienced passion in their own relationships.

Wondering about me, are you? Yes, I will admit, I am one of the lucky ones. I have experienced unbridled passion. Unfortunately, he is long gone and with another, but the memories are as hot as ever.

Why is it that we do not find more passion in our relationships? Seems like the only place a woman can find it these days is inside the pages a romance novel. Passion is something we all want to experience, but few ever experience the emotion first hand. We dream about it, wish for it, or lose it afterward.

It is definitely a transient emotion—hard to find and hard to keep. It is a fire that ignites and dies, and I wonder why. Perhaps it is our own fault. We do not know how to start the fire, and apparently, we don't know how to keep it burning either.

(Posted Sunday, May 18, 2008)

Seduction

"Music so terrible it consumes all those who approach it."
Gaston Leroux

Let's attend an opera and listen to the musical score the Phantom has written—"Don Juan Triumphant."

What is the strange opera that the Phantom writes? Who is Don Juan anyway? If you are not familiar with the story, Don Juan (or *Don Giovanni* in other adaptations) is a legendary fictional tale about a libertine (a term for a man who is morally or sexually unrestrained). He enjoys fights, rapes and seduces women.

In the story, he seduces a woman from a noble family and kills her father. The ghost of the father invites him to dine with him in the cemetery. Don Juan accepts the offer. Tricked into shaking the hand of a statue, he finds himself pulled by him and dragged into hell.

The Phantom's title, however, is "Don Juan Triumphant." It is his declaration he will triumph in his conquest and seduction over Christine. As you first listen to the opera, the music is very chaotic in nature. Even the audience looks at one another and wonders about the odd musical score.

The music, I think, is a statement of the chaotic agony within the Phantom's mind. However, later he uses his composition as a means of seduction. Christine is his prey, and he leads her into a trap.

The Phantom in Leroux warns Christine about the power of the music in "Don Juan Triumphant":

"'*Will you play me something out of your Don Juan Triumphant?' I asked, thinking to please him. 'You must never ask me that,' he said, in a gloomy voice. 'I will play you Mozart, if you like, which will only make you weep; but my Don Juan, Christine, burns . . .'*"

Erik cleverly composes lyrics for Christine to sing. She finds the piece intoxicating, as she confesses in song her deepest unspoken desires and passions for Erik. In return, he sings to her seducing her into the trap, even though he is in danger of capture. He risks everything to express his deepest desire for her.

Remember the scene in the 2004 movie? At the end of the song, for a brief moment, Christine lays against his chest caressed in his loving embrace. Everything around has disappeared, except the man who now holds her in his arms. As we all know, she comes to her senses and turns around and betrays him instead. As a result, he takes her by force and drags her back to his lair.

Seduction is a powerful tool used to trap and ensnare, and as we can see, Erik used it to his advantage. Again, it suggests the analogy of Satan, for he is the seducer and deceiver who attempts to drag unsuspecting humanity into hell by the means of seduction and deceit.

(POSTED SUNDAY, FEBRUARY 17, 2008)

Section Three

Symbols in the Phantom of the Opera

Angel of Music
Box 5
Chandelier
Graveyard
Lasso
Mask
Mirrors
Music
Music Box
Red Death
Ring
Rose
Tears
Trap Doors

Angel of Music

*"The Angel of Music played a part in all
Daddy Daaé's tales . . . "*
Gaston Leroux

Who is the Angel of Music anyway? Why did Erik call himself an Angel of Music? Why did Christine seek the Angel of Music?

When we equate Erik to darkness, we see the story symbolizes him as a type of Satan. The name Erik means eternal ruler. Satan is the eternal ruler of darkness. Christine's name means disciple of Christ, follower of Christ, or Christ-like. Do you think Leroux picked those names for a purpose to make a point or they were purely coincidental?

If you are wondering why Christine was so adamant about her father sending to her the Angel of Music, that explanation stems from Leroux's version. Her father told her that the Angel of Music at least once in life visited every great musician, and when he arrived in heaven, he promised that he would send the Angel of Music.

The Phantom pretends to be the Angel of Music to Christine. Of course, we know he calls himself the Angel of Hell. He deceives Christine into thinking he is the Angel of Music sent by her father to tutor her.

In comparison, Satan, or Lucifer is described in the Bible as once being the anointed cherub, an angel of music, who because of pride was cast out of heaven becoming the great deceiver and murderer of humanity. Do you see the similarities?

The Phantom uses this deception to lure Christine into his world of darkness bidding her come to the Angel of Music. She thinks he is an Angel of light when in fact he's the Angel of darkness. In the end, Christine cries that he deceived her. When the Phantom allows Christine and Raoul to leave, he declares once again that he is the Angel of Hell.

The symbolism is there, yet that is not the end of the story. I do not believe that Erik is eternally doomed to a life in hell. On the contrary, it is not the life in hell he longs for, it's the life of beauty and redemption.

Erik learns about redemption through one simple act, which is the laying down of one's life for another. All three of our characters end up doing the same.

Raoul lays down his life to save Christine. Christine lays down her life to save Raoul. Erik sacrifices and learns the meaning of love by laying down his life's desire to keep Christine. Instead, he gives her freedom. Redemption has touched his heart, and he learns the meaning of true compassion and love.

If we are not careful, we can be victims of deception, just like the Angel of Music deceived Christine.

(POSTED SUNDAY, JANUARY 27, 2008)

Box 5

"It's Box Five, you know, the box on the grand tier, next to the stage-box, on the left."
Gaston Leroux

Box 5, the Phantom's requested seat in the opera house. Did he demand Box 5 because it is the best seat in the house? Did he enjoy that secret entrance that allowed him to come and go at will? What deeper symbolism is in Box 5 if any? After all, the Phantom demanded the box be reserved for his use alone and not shared with another.

If you research the number five, you will find many symbolic meanings attributed to the numeric symbol. Here are a few:
- Biblical interpretation relates the number five to bondage or prison.
- The musical staff has five lines.
- There is a five-petal rose.
- The pentagram has five sides (representation of magic or Lucifer).
- Humans have five senses.
- The Opera Ghost lived five stories under the opera house.

Is the box just about the number or does it

have a deeper meaning? If the opera house was the Phantom's domain since childhood and he the ultimate ruler of it, was Box 5 a symbol of his throne of authority and dominion? From his seat in Box 5, he could see the stage, Christine, and the domain of his power and control. When Raoul sat in his box, he reiterated that Box 5 was to be left empty.

Assuredly, Raoul seated in the Phantom's box was a threatening act, a sign that Raoul was usurping the Phantom's claim, invading his territory, and gaining power over Christine. His domain was under attack, his throne threatened. Was that the reason why in the next scene he kills to reassert his authority over his domain?

Perhaps if the Phantom were here, we could enter his darkened mind and ask the true reason why he insisted on Box 5, or maybe we know already. Can you think of any other reason?

For curious minds who wish to know, there are fans who have visited Box 5 at the Opera Garnier in Paris. Some swear they can feel a lingering presence. It's too bad we all can't go to Paris and find out for ourselves what the view is like from Box 5.

(POSTED MONDAY, JANUARY 28, 2008)

Chandelier

"Lot 666"
Referenced in the Webber Stage Version

Symbolism abounds in the lot number, as well as the chandelier representing light and darkness.

Probably the most obvious reference to darkness is the number 666, which is the lot number used to identify the chandelier at auction. It's the Biblical reference in Revelations attributed to the mark of beast or Satan:

"*This calls for wisdom. If anyone has insight, let him calculate the number of the beast, for it is man's number. His number is 666.*" (Revelation 13:18).

What does the Lot 666 resemble for the Phantom? Frankly, I think it pertains to his lot in life assigned by fate, which is one to live in a world of darkness and rejection. When he drags Christine back down to his world in his last attempt to possess her as his own, he takes her down that path to darkness and hell.

On the other hand, the chandelier is a grand representation of light before its destruction. The crystal light fixture illuminates the world of the Opera Populaire at the height of its grandeur, even though it subsequently becomes a chandelier in pieces. Our dear Phantom succeeds in ultimately destroying the beauty of the world he loves so much and plunges the opera house into darkness and burning fire; again, another type of hell.

I really like the auction's symbolism. For here, we see the chandelier for sale. It is clean, refitted with the new electric light, repaired, and ready for sale to the highest bidder. When the auctioneer says "gentlemen," they pull the rope and hoist the chandelier once again. The chandelier pleas for someone to resurrect it from the darkness, and begs for restoration to the former glory it once knew. We see another example of redemption in the process.

What lesson can we draw? Perhaps, your lot in life is not one you like. Are you looking for someone to redeem you from the darkness and resurrect you into a new life? Let your mind wander through the symbolism of the lot number and the chandelier and see where it leads you.

(POSTED SUNDAY, JANUARY 27, 2008)

Graveyard

"Raoul walked away, dejectedly, to the graveyard in which the church stood and was indeed alone among the tombs, reading the inscriptions . . ."
Gaston Leroux

Have you ever walked through a graveyard? Let's take a walk through the one in *The Phantom of the Opera*. Just like Christine, we will pass sculpted angels and stone figures that surround the path. Try to imagine a chilling white mist swirling around your feet, and cold snow falling softly on your body. Death is everywhere around you.

Why is Christine here? What woeful song does she sing as she proceeds through the icy darkness toward her father's crypt? What deception lays waiting to entice her once again? Let's see if we can uncover meaning in the soulful trek she takes and why the Phantom waits for her in the graveyard.

Leroux penned that Christine was orphaned at a young age, having *"lost with the death of her father her voice, her soul, and her genius,"* only to discover it again after the Angel of Music visits her. The Phantom becomes her tutor, her guide, and she finds solace and protection in the Angel of Music in the absence of her father's care. She trusts the Angel of Music blindly because she believes her father has sent him to her as he promised. Only now, as she stands before her father's crypt, she knows there is no angel, but a man who she both admires and fears.

Christine is at the crossroads of her life. She's about to marry Raoul. She realizes, with grief, that to take the next step, she must learn to bury her past and let go of her dead father. Therefore, in a symbolic gesture, she goes to the graveyard and sings a song of goodbye, asking for strength to move on without him.

The Phantom, however, sees Christine emerging into maturity and moving farther away from her reliance upon him as her teacher. In a desperate attempt to ensnare her once again, he calls to her. Suddenly reality is blurred. Is it her father calling? Is it the Angel of Music? Is it Phantom or friend? The Phantom, with his angelic and enticing voice, attempts to draw her back under his control. He knows her weakness. He plays upon her childlike trust, devotion, and yearning for her father until Raoul arrives to awaken her from the trance.

Christine struggles with the promise her father made. She believes he sent the Angel of Music, but now knows it is the Phantom instead. Does she struggle to let go of not only her father, but also the Phantom to whom she owes so much? He is the one who taught her to sing. He alone gave back her voice and inspiration that died with the death of her father. As she pleads for Raoul to spare his life, we see that Christine is not ready to let go of Erik, who she owes so much. He is the only Angel of Music she has known.

What can we learn from Christine's symbolic walk through the graveyard? I believe there are times we too need to take a symbolic walk ourselves in the graveyard of life, to leave things behind that hinder us from reaching a new level of maturity. All of us experience, broken dreams, hurts, and emotions that we need to let go and bury. If we do not lay aside what hinders us, we will never reach a new level in our lives and be able to move on. Instead, we doom ourselves to a life that is an emotional graveyard of cold monuments and ghosts that forever remind and haunt us of our past.

Do you need to take a walk through the graveyard? If so, take a stroll, bury the past and move on. You will be a better person.

(POSTED SATURDAY, FEBRUARY 9, 2008)

Lasso

"No one knows better than he how to throw the Punjab lasso, for he is the king of stranglers..."
Gaston Leroux

We are going to examine the dark side of Erik and talk about one of his skills that earned him the title of "king of stranglers."

Occasionally, I get an email with the question what does the term *"keep your hand at the level of your eyes"* mean? It comes from Leroux's version, where the Persian tells Raoul about Erik's uncanny skill of being able to strangle his victims with his Punjab lasso.

Apparently, Erik learned this skill while living in abroad. He practiced his art by strangling men condemned to death in front of applauding audiences. Of course, we know this is how poor Joseph Buquet ends up swinging from the catwalk above, from the lasso made out of catgut. Erik was carrying out an execution.

Madame Giry warns both Joseph Buquet and Raoul de Chagny to keep their hands at the level of their eyes if they encounter the Phantom. Why? As explained by the Persian to Raoul, this is the only means of protection for an intended victim. When the lasso is swung around one's neck, if your arm is up and the hand at the level of your eye, it catches both the arm and the neck, thereby allowing you to loosen the lasso and go free. Listen up and remember that little tip next time you are walking around uninvited in the opera cellars.

Did Joseph or Raoul listen to the advice? Well, the answer is obvious. I bet they wished they had while they were hanging from the end of a rope. One died for his mistake, and the other almost died, all because they did not heed the warning.

Raoul forgot. Instead, he let his guard down only to end up caught by the Phantom's rope. In a moment of weakness, Erik took advantage. Stress and danger in our lives can often cloud our ability to think straight or act defensively, and so was the case with Raoul.

Let's be honest. Life is filled with warnings how to escape danger, which we often forget, ignore, or do not take to heart. We let our guard down, get distracted, and end up in trouble. We make poor choices under duress and put ourselves at risk.

Had Raoul taken the warning seriously and kept his eyes on the Phantom the entire time by keeping his hands at the level of his eyes, it would not have given Erik the upper hand. Instead, he put himself into an uncomfortable position of strangulation.

Life is tough enough without allowing it to strangle the life out of us, so pay attention, and keep your hand at the level of your eyes.

(POSTED SATURDAY, JANUARY 31, 2009)

Mask

"I have invented a mask that makes me look like anybody."
Gaston Leroux

The mask embodies so much symbolism that I will never be able to touch all aspects of its meaning in one article. You will see that I refer to its existence in others, as well as the agony that we find behind Erik's mask. I know Erik hates his mask removed revealing the ugliness underneath, but for this article, we really need to peek and see what's there.

The mask's purpose is obvious. Erik uses it to hide his deformity and make his appearance more appealing. In the book, the Phantom states, *"I have invented a mask that makes me look like anybody."*

In the movie version, I dare say most women would agree that the movie star chosen, played an extremely handsome and attractive masked Phantom. Of course, isn't that the point of our masks anyway? To hide what is ugly and painful inside and allow us to play a more loveable and desirable role to find acceptance?

Christine is a curious woman. She wants to know what is behind the mask. She feels the need to see beneath it, to reveal the hidden face. Seeking to see what is there, she removes the Phantom's mask without asking permission. In doing so, the Phantom cries out in grief and rage as that hideous part of his life is painfully exposed. (*See Note Below*)

As human beings, we all yearn for love and acceptance, but as a rule we are not transparent. We all wear masks to protect ourselves from exposure. Frankly, humanity has been hiding behind masks since the Garden of Eden. Sure, it was a fig leaf for Adam and Eve, but the concept is the same. We are afraid of our emotional nakedness, so we hide ourselves.

We all live behind masks that cover our deepest hurts and darkest thoughts. For someone to pull our mask off uninvited and gaze at what is underneath is a painful experience. We would react in embarrassment and anger like the Phantom. Our masks don't necessarily hide a physical deformity. Instead, they hide the painful emotional dimensions of our lives from the world.

Most of us would agree it is easier to keep our mask on than to take it off and risk exposure. It takes great courage to remove your mask and reveal your true self to another person. When you do so, you risk rejection. Once rejected, like the Phantom, we tend to pick up the mask, place it back on our face, and continue with our lives none the better.

Stories like *The Phantom of the Opera* wouldn't continue to touch so many hearts if we lived in a world where acceptance and love were normal behavior. Millions relate to Erik's pain.

Sadly, human nature is cruel and superficial, and perhaps it takes a divine nature to love and accept us unconditionally.

Do I wear a mask? Of course, I do. It hides my deepest hurts and the rejection I have experienced throughout life. I dare say it will take some doing to remove mine, and I kindly request you do not attempt to remove it without my permission.

(POSTED SUNDAY, FEBRUARY 3, 2008)

NOTE: THIS CRITICAL SCENE HAS BEEN REMOVED FROM *THE PHANTOM OF THE OPERA* NORTH AMERICAN TOUR. CHRISTINE NO LONGER REMOVES HIS MASK ON HER OWN. SHE AWAKENS TO FIND HIM UNMASKED.

Mirrors

*"She herself was moving to the back of the room, the whole
wall of which was occupied by a great mirror
hat reflected her image . . ."*
Gaston Leroux

Throughout the stage rendition and the original novel, the symbolic use of mirrors abounds, but more so in the original book. Nevertheless, let us look at the reflection in the mirror and see what is there.

A mirror is any smooth, shiny surface that forms an image by reflection. When we gaze into a mirror, our reflection returns to us, and we see ourselves through our own eyes. The reflection we see is either reality or distortion, depending upon how our brain translates the picture. Psychiatry defines a body image distortion disorder for those who look in the mirror and see themselves as something they are not. The image reflected in the mirror and our perception of that image, produces a profound effect on our behavior.

Christine faces the mirror in her dressing room. The mirror calls for her to explore the depths of the Phantom and the one who has forged her inner self through his music. Through the mirror, he calls her and bids her look at her own image.

What she discovers in the mirror is the reflection of the Phantom, who has become part of her, dwelling inside her mind, and now bids her into his world to know him. She succumbs, and in a trance-like state follows him through the mirror to his domain.

In the book, the Phantom's torture chamber is a room of mirrors representing the true torture of his own life, which is his reflection. In the movie, we see the mirrors in his lair hidden and covered. Christine removes his mask, and he runs to a mirror and pulls off its covering asking her if this is what she wanted to see. The mirror reflects not only his ugliness, but also the agony of his soul.

However, the mirrors have deeper meanings behind them. As humans, we are visually driven and attracted toward outward beauty, which we highly value in others and in ourselves. We often fail to understand that the essence of who we are reaches far beyond our outward appearance. Beauty is also an inward quality, and Christine points out where the true distortion in his personality lies.

How often do you look in a mirror and find displeasure in what you see? What image reflects back into your eyes? Is it pleasing or torturous? Do you see self-worth or self-disdain?

Your image, however, reaches far beyond the reflection of the mirror; it goes to the depth of your soul. Your body will waste away in the grave, but your soul and its essence will continue throughout eternity. Would it not be a better to focus on the eternal within us, rather than to agonize over that which is temporal and wasting away?

Go to a mirror and tell me what you see. Let the reflection come back into your eyes through the window of your soul. If you see some distortion within, perhaps it is time to acknowledge its existence, pick up the candlestick, and break the mirror as the Phantom did. You can leave the ugliness of your distorted soul behind and walk through to new life.

(POSTED SATURDAY, FEBRUARY 2, 2008)

Music

"You see, Christine, there is some music that is so terrible that it consumes all those who approach it."
Gaston Leroux

What is music? Where does it come from? How is it inspired? The word music is a Greek word derived from "mousa" or "muse." In Greek mythology, Muses were a sisterhood of goddesses or spirits, who embodied the arts and inspired creation in song, stage, writing, music, and dance.

Music has the innate power to touch the depths of our souls and cause emotion to well up inside of our hearts. It changes the way we feel and behave. It elicits a whole gambit of emotions: joy, exuberances, sadness, melancholy, inspiration, motivation, rest, beauty, and healing—just to name a few.

The Bible speaks of the power of music in I Samuel 16:23:

"*Whenever the spirit from God came upon Saul, David would take his harp and play. Then relief would come to Saul; he would feel better, and the evil spirit would leave him.*"

Have you ever heard the statement, *"music*

has charms to soothe the savage beast?"[5] Perhaps that is why the Phantom received the gift of musical genius—to soothe the savage beast within.

Erik understands the power of his gift, and he uses it to his advantage. Music is his tool to touch Christine's mind and spirit. With music, he can entice and seduce. He takes Christine to his lair and asks that she sing for him. He shares with Christine his musical genius, and she confesses to Raoul how his music touched her soul.

Musical creation comes from the heart, molded by strong emotion. Andrew Lloyd Webber uses music to touch us with the story of *The Phantom of the Opera*, by composing a powerful and haunting musical score to tell Erik's story. Frankly, I think it's genius that the genius of music is immortalized in a musical!

Has the musical score of *The Phantom of the Opera* touched your heart? I dare say most of us have memorized a few of our favorite songs. I never grow weary of the musical score by Andrew Lloyd Webber or the poignant lyrics woven by Charles Hart and Richard Stilgoe. They are gifted musical geniuses, and I thank them for the wonderful stage production.

(POSTED WEDNESDAY, FEBRUARY 6, 2008)

Music Box

"A collector's piece . . ."
Referenced in the Webber Stage Version

The music box! Cute little toy. Why does the Phantom keep a music box anyway? It's not exactly what I would consider very manly.

There is no mention of a music box in Leroux's work. It is a creation of the stage play and is a monkey in Persian robes playing the cymbals to the song "Masquerade." The Persian in the book was someone who knew Erik very well. He was aware of Erik's past life, and Erik confided in him.

What fascinates me the most about the music box, as portrayed in the play, is the act of Raoul purchasing it at auction. The strange deed piques my imagination and opens up a world of possibilities regarding Christine's subsequent life with Raoul. The movie does not give us an answer. It teases our imagination to wonder why Raoul, who fought so hard to free her, buys a memento of her captivity with the Phantom and leaves it at her grave.

What is my interpretation? I think Raoul knew throughout his life with Christine, that though she married him, part of her heart always belonged to the Phantom. Raoul, now after Christine's death, decides to acknowledge her longing for her former tutor by leaving at her grave a valued possession belonging to his nemesis.

What climax the scene holds that after this selfless act of giving her the music box, he is astonished to see the Phantom's rose and the engagement ring on Christine's gravestone. It seems like the Phantom has left his own parting gift for Christine, at Raoul's startled surprise. It's a poignant picture of two men loving the same woman, and each giving her a gift in honor of their love.

(POSTED TUESDAY, JANUARY 29, 2008)

Red Death

"Don't touch me! I am Red Death stalking abroad!"
Gaston Leroux

This should be an easy post for all of us required to read classic literature. Edgar Allen Poe's story entitled, *The Masque of the Red Death* [6] was no doubt on your reading list in high school. For those of you who have not read the classic tale and wonder why the movie version Phantom looks so darn hot in that red outfit during the masquerade, this article will enlighten you on the symbolism of the costume. (*See Note Below*)

Okay, get out your notepad and pick up a pen. We are going on a journey. Remember, this is how I view that dastardly, but strikingly handsome man, dressed in red. You might have an entirely different view, so I encourage you, as always, to think about the symbolism.

If someone were to ask me to come up with two words to describe Red Death, I would use the term "party crasher." In Poe's story, Leroux's book, and the stage and movie version, that is just what the Phantom is doing. He is a party crasher to make deadly and gruesome point.

The Masque of Red Death told a tale of a horrible plague killing its victims with pain, dizziness, and bleeding from the pores, and understandably, a ghastly death, swift, and feared by many.

Poe's describes a Prince, who is "happy and dauntless and sagacious." After losing half his population to the plague of Red Death, he hides behind the doors of a fortress, which he thinks is impenetrable from the disease. He fills his locked castle with merry friends, who do not have the time to grieve or think of the horrors outside. The Prince provides his guests will all the pleasures they need, such as musicians, merriment, food, and wine. The Prince and his friends lack compassion for those perishing outside their walls and block out their thought with pleasures by celebrating. They are smug, proud and believe they cannot be touched.

After six months of lockdown in seclusion, while humankind continues to die from the plague outside the walls, the Prince decides to hold a Masque Ball. He oddly decorates seven suites in which to party, all decorated in various colors, beautiful and bizarre in their own way. The seventh and last room he decorates in the color of red, with a clock that chimes ominously on the hour throughout the night.

The party begins. Everybody dresses for the Masque Ball. All the guests drink, party, and have a good time until an uninvited stranger crashes the party dressed as follows:

"*The figure was tall and gaunt, and shrouded from head to foot in the habiliments of the grave.*

The mask which concealed the visage was made so nearly to resemble the countenance of a stiffened corpse that the closest scrutiny must have had difficulty in detecting the cheat. And yet all this might have been endured, if not approved, by the mad revelers around. But the mummer had gone so far as to assume the type of the Red Death. His vesture was dabbled in blood–and his broad brow, with all the features of the face, was besprinkled with the scarlet horror."

The crowd wonders about this masquerader. The Prince sees him dressed like Red Death, and is enraged at his mocking appearance. He tries to stab the figure with a dagger and falls dead at his feet in the seventh room decorated in red. The remaining crowd grabs at the figure and finds there is no tangible form underneath, and at the stroke of Midnight, they all succumb to the deadly plague of Red Death and drop dead too. Poe ends with this chilling statement:

"*And Darkness and Decay and the Red Death held illimitable dominion over all.*"

Equality has arrived.

So why did the Phantom show up to the masquerade dressed as Red Death? Why in the world did he choose to identify himself with the story written by Edgar Allen Poe? I see a variety of similarities and one striking undertone in the message.

First, just like Red Death, he is an uninvited guest. No one wants him there in the first place. The crowd revels at their party singing there is no more ghost, no more notes, all is quiet. The guests don't have a care in the world until the Opera

Ghost appears and steps down the stairway infiltrating their party uninvited.

Second, everyone at the masquerade is dressed in beautiful finery, hiding behind their masks, with faces of beauty, wearing costumes of beauty, reveling in their fun. Enter the Phantom dressed as Red Death. Leroux describes his outfit as:

"... *a person whose disguise, eccentric air and gruesome appearance were causing a sensation. It was a man dressed all in scarlet, with a huge hat and feathers on the top of a wonderful death's head. From his shoulders hung an immense red-velvet cloak, which trailed along the floor like a king's train; and on this cloak was embroidered, in gold letters, which everyone read and repeated aloud, "Don't touch me! I am Red Death stalking abroad!"*

What is the Opera Ghost doing here uninvited dressed like Red Death? He's making a point that no one is immune from death, and this fact is the one common ground he shares with all the revelers at the Masque Ball. Death holds dominion over all. No matter how hard they try to escape, no one escapes death. Their class systems will be gone, their riches will be left behind, their titles, possessions, intelligence will not buy them reprieve. Their beauty and perfection will fade and rot in the grave among the worms. Here the Opera Ghost is like everyone else, as gruesome as the thought might be to the unsuspecting crowd.

An interesting statement Leroux pens from Erik's lips:

"*I want to live like everybody else. I want to*

have a wife like everybody else and to take her out on Sundays. I have invented a mask that makes me look like anybody."

Again, we hear the cry of his heart. You have left him outside, locked the doors, and given him no compassion or thought. If he cannot have commonality with you in life, then he wants you to know, he will have it in death.

What do you see in the story of Red Death? Yes, the Phantom is quite handsome in his red outfit and white mask in the movie version. He has not slipped into that costume, however, to make you swoon over his good looks. On the contrary, he just wants you to know that darkness, decay, and death bind you together.

(POSTED MONDAY, DECEMBER 15, 2008)

NOTE: THE RED DEATH COSTUME HAS CHANGED FROM THE ORIGINAL STAGE PLAY. IN THE NORTH AMERICAN TOUR, IT CLOSELY MATCHES THE COSTUME WORN IN THE 2004 MOVIE VERSION.

Ring

"The next day, he saw her at the Opera. She was still wearing the plain gold ring."
Gaston Leroux

The geometrical design of a ring is an age-old symbol of eternity; a never-ending connotation. Have you ever noticed the number of things in nature represented by rings or circles? The rings around planets, the orbits around the sun, the moon circling the earth, the circle of bird's nest, the cycle of life interwoven in circles in the things we do. The ring is endless, timeless, repetitive, and an unbroken circle that is filled with symbolism.

Throughout history, weddings use the symbol of the ring not only to indicate eternity, but also to indicate possession. The ring, given by the husband, indicates he possesses the wife, and she is no longer available to other men. We see the ring used in The Phantom of the Opera in both the original work and the movie as a symbol of possession. However, if you watch its journey, you will see the ring make a full circle, but never lives out its intended purpose.

In the book, the Phantom gives Christine a

plain gold wedding band to wear. Historically, gold bands were a symbol the bridegroom trusted his betrothed with his valuable property, and society considered it good luck for the wife to wear a gold band rather than silver. The Phantom tells Christine:

"*On condition that this ring is always on your finger. As long as you keep it, you will be protected against all danger and Erik will remain your friend.*"

When Raoul sees the ring, he knows it signifies the Phantom's possession of her as his future wife, but Christine loses the ring. When the Phantom releases her, he gives her the ring back as a wedding gift. *"I held in my hand a ring, a plain gold ring which I had given her."* The Phantom her gives her the ring back when he releases Christine, as a wedding present to her and Raoul. At his request upon his death, she returns to Erik and places the plain gold ring back on his finger. The ring has made a full circle.

In the movie, we see a different version. Raoul gives Christine an engagement ring. Only this ring is a beautiful piece of jewelry, not a plain gold wedding band. In high society, the quality of the jewelry given to a woman indicated the social position and prosperity of the groom. Perhaps this is why Webber's version uses a diamond ring.

The Phantom, however, after seeing the ring, tears it from Christine's neck, reiterating his continued possession of her. She does not belong to Raoul. He steals the ring, as he plots to steal her. After he brings her to his lair, he gives her the ring in anticipation of marriage. She puts the ring on her finger, agrees to become his wife. When the Phantom frees her to leave with Raoul, she takes the ring off, and she gives it back to him once again. He carries it throughout life until her death and returns it to her grave. Once again, the ring has made a full circle.

The ring no doubt is a symbol of possession in the story, and the Phantom's desire to possess Christine for eternity. However, as hard as he schemes to win her love, he never fully possesses her heart. The ring never lives out its intended purpose as a symbol of eternity. It only makes a full circle and comes back to him, and Erik returns to a life of solitude.

If you wear a wedding ring on your finger, take a moment and ponder its meaning. Be thankful you have someone in your life that possesses your heart. There are those of us, like Erik, whose rings have made a full circle. No one possesses our hearts now, and we, like him, have returned to a life of solitude.

(POSTED TUESDAY, FEBRUARY 12, 2008)

Rose

*"They were marvelous red roses that had blossomed
in the morning . . ."*
Gaston Leroux

The rose is a beautiful flower. It's been adored throughout history as a flower of romance. We write songs and poems about roses. We hold tournaments and parades in its honor. We crush its fragrant petals to make perfume. The rose is the flower of choice that you give to someone you love, as the Phantom did with a black ribbon tied around its stem in the movie version. Red roses symbolize passion and love.

As beautiful as the rose appears, it contains a hidden darkness. If you do not handle it carefully in its beauty, it can cause great pain. How interesting that nature has designed a flower so beautiful to look upon but so painful to the touch. Has nature left a message in creation that as beautiful as romantic love can be, it can contain a thorn to pierce our hearts as well?

In *The Phantom of the Opera* movie, Christine carries the red rose he has given her to the rooftop. After she declares her love for Raoul, she drops the rose in the cold snow. Erik picks up

From the Phantom of the Opera

the discarded symbol of his love and feels the thorn of rejection in the beauty of the rose. Rejection does not always drive us to madness, as it did the Phantom, but it can drive us to heartbreak that is practically unbearable.

Rejection from someone we love is no doubt the most powerful emotional pain any individual can experience. Perhaps you have felt the thorn of rejection as well.

What can we say about the passion of love? Do we learn to handle it carefully, overwhelmed by its beauty and aroma, but always cautious that we never use its thorn to pierce another person's heart? If we have already been the victim of its pierce, how do we overcome the hurt and pain? There is no right answer or counsel for a broken heart or rejection from the one we love. Does time heal all wounds? Perhaps. Do we need to carry the hurt forever? Not necessarily. Does the pain eventually subside? Slowly it dissipates over time as my own experience has taught me.

Perhaps we should learn another lesson from the rose. After the rose fades, its petals fall, and it has been pruned and remains dormant throughout the winter of our lives, eventually it will bloom again in spring more beautiful than before.

The next time a rose blooms in your life, may it bring to you only beauty and no pain.

(Posted Saturday January 26, 2008)

have mingled your tears with his pain and felt compassion.

(POSTED MONDAY FEBRUARY 4, 2008)

Trapdoors

*"I am a trapdoor lover, and I open and shut what
I please and as I please."*
Gaston Leroux

What was Erik's fixation with trapdoors all about? It is an odd hobby, building trapdoors everywhere to trip and trap unsuspecting individuals.

Magicians and illusionists use trapdoors as tools of their trade, as well as stage productions. Leroux's version deals heavily with trapdoors, more so than the stage play or movie. In the movie, there are some trapdoors. We see the Phantom utilize a trap door in the masquerade scene. He makes his dramatic exit, and Raoul drops down the hole to follow. The Phantom uses a trap door on the stage to abduct Christine, and poor Raoul nearly perishes falling through a trap door into the water.

Trapdoors were the entrance to Erik's underworld, his kingdom, and domain. The doors had duel purposes. The first was to trap and harm those who would dare to enter his world; and the second, a tool for his own use to come and go unseen. His involvement in the architecture and building of the opera house afforded him the opportunity to incorporate numerous hidden doors only he knew existed.

Once again, as the Phantom equates himself as an Angel of Hell, you can see the familiar analogy. The Bible describes Satan as a master of deceit and disguise, setting traps to ensnare unsuspecting humanity.

The Phantom uses trapdoors as tools to bring unsuspecting individuals into torture chambers. One described in the book is entirely of mirrors, as the one portrayed in the movie, designed to create madness in the minds of its victims trapped within its walls. How interesting that he uses mirrors to torture others, for no doubt each time he gazes into a mirror, he tortures his own soul.

When I speak of the Phantom, I know many of you conjure images of a handsome movie star, but in Leroux, our Phantom possesses a dark side. The Persian calls him a monster and describes what horrors he is capable of inflicting upon others. Fans tend to romanticize *The Phantom of the Opera* greatly, and I too am guilty as charged. However, the story does portray a darker side of the Phantom and the evils he is capable of inflicting upon others. He tortures; he murders.

How do I deal with such stark reality regarding the darker side of Erik? I find relief in sequels to *The Phantom of the Opera*, many of which bring him to a point of redemption. The stories tend to lead him out of darkness and into the light of the world where he finally finds love and acceptance. It's just another human quality we can apply to our favorite story, which is our desire to find redemption from the darkness in our lives.

(POSTED SATURDAY, NOVEMBER 8, 2008)

Section Four
Events, Places & Things in the Phantom of the Opera

Betrayal
Illusion
Lair
Masquerade
Opera

Betrayal

"I hope, M. de Chagny," he said, "that you have not betrayed Erik's secret."
Gaston Leroux

One cannot talk about Christine without talking about her act of betrayal, which is a pivotal point in the story. Her betrayal happens at two points, one on the rooftop and second at the "Point of No Return." Why did she betray the Phantom? Erik asks her why. Christine is silent, however, and has no words to defend her actions.

Christine, why are you so silent? Why did you do it? Inquiring minds wish to know!

In the movie, on the rooftop, Christine drops the rose and chooses a life with Raoul out of fear of the Phantom. Unknowing to her, Erik is in the shadows watching her choice and afterward cries from the pain of rejection, angry over how she has betrayed him after he inspired her voice.

I do not believe that Christine was consciously thinking of betrayal at that moment. It was more of an unconscious move away from the Phantom's influence and a leaning toward Raoul's protection. Because of her actions though, the thorn of rejection pierces Erik's heart.

The second betrayal, of course, is more of a conscious decision made by Christine. In the chapel, we see her confusion. She struggles at the thought of betraying the one who inspired her voice but remembers he kills without a thought, as well. She believes betrayal is the only way to purchase her freedom from his obsession, but on the other hand wishes she could refuse. Christine is conflicted and torn but decides to sing the Phantom's Opera. She also recognizes that even if she betrays him, he will always be there singing songs in her head and never truly free.

In the movie, at the "Point of No Return," there is a subtle betrayal also played out between Christine and Raoul. There is no doubt that Christine has an attraction to the Phantom. She struggles with her attraction for a brief moment at the "Point of No Return." She leans against Erik's chest, he caresses her tenderly in his arms, and she loses herself in his embrace. Raoul watches but is sickened at the sight of her reaction in the arms of his enemy.

When Erik asks Christine the ultimate question to spend the rest of her life with him, she awakens to a reality that she is not willing to accept. She answers with an act of betrayal. Christine knew what was behind the mask, and she knew the violent reaction it would elicit from Erik when she stripped it from his face. Christine did the unthinkable to buy her freedom, which was the price she was willing to pay. However, in stripping the Phantom's mask off, she strips him of his last ounce of dignity and exposes that most vulnerable and painful part of his humanity to his enemies. Frankly, it was cruel.

Erik's pain is unimaginable when betrayal comes at the hand of the woman he loves. It cuts him deeply and only further leads him down the path of madness to take what he so desperately wants.

What about Raoul? He played his own part in Christine's betrayal in forcing her to perform the Phantom's Opera. As I keep pondering his act of buying the Phantom's music box at auction and taking it to her grave, I keep asking myself for what purpose? At auction, he pays thirty francs for the music box, which is the age-old symbol of the price of betrayal—thirty pieces of silver.

What can we learn from this horrid act of betrayal? As much as we wish Christine had chosen a life with Erik, the story remains unchanged. There are no alternate endings on the DVD. At least I have not found one on the menu option. Many fans would prefer Erik living happily ever after with Christine. To soften the blow, we imagine alternate endings to satisfy how we would prefer the final act. We write sequels to quench our thirst for different outcomes, which works fairly well to change the sad ending that may be too painful for fans to accept. Perhaps we equate sad ending to our own life experiences, and that is why we so desperately wish to rewrite the story.

However, real life gives no edit option. We must live with the consequences of our actions, whether good or bad. All our acts play out. We cannot go back and rewrite chapters or provide for ourselves alternate endings to painful moments. Each chapter in our lives is an unchangeable story penned in eternal ink. As we make our choices, we must remember that our acts not only play out in our own lives, but they inherently touch those close to us.

No doubt, Raoul realized that Erik's voice still sang songs in Christine's head throughout her life. Why else would he purchase the music box to place on her grave? A music box he thought would still be playing after all of them were dead.

(POSTED FRIDAY, MARCH 14, 2008)

Illusion

"The Opera Ghost really existed."
Gaston Leroux

A few years ago, I braved the world of roleplaying as Christine Daaé. If you want to roleplay *The Phantom of the Opera*, you pretty much need a profile as the Phantom or Christine to get any attention on a social media site.

If you are not familiar with roleplaying, most role players are anonymous. You never know whom you are playing with at the other end of the cyber network. Frankly, I was terrified to try this form of entertainment, but pushed myself during the months I was taking an advanced fiction writing class. My instructor even encouraged the behavior as an excellent way to keep my pen flowing every day by forcing myself to write character and storyline. I met some amazing writers who penned circles around me; and, frankly, I think they are much too tolerant of my dabbling in the area of fiction. (It paid off, because as of this 3rd edition, I have since written nine other fiction books.)

Do I enjoy it? Yes, but I'm cautious. It certainly

brings you into a world of illusion—a make-believe place that is not real. I suck my brain into Christine's body. I love her body and looks but am not too keen on her brain. I am molding my Christine differently. She is not the Christine I have dissected in my articles, who used and betrayed two men.

Roleplaying has taught me that illusion is a powerful medium of control. It can take you to a place that brings strange comfort but also great danger. After reading enough psychology articles on the subject, I have come close to throwing in my pen afraid I will take the entire world I have created too seriously. So why do I continue? I find a strange comfort in a make-believe world. While surfing the Internet, I found a very interesting quote by Jean Cocteau that speaks of illusion:

"Man seeks to escape himself in myth and does so by any means at his disposal. Drugs, alcohol, or lies. Unable to withdraw into himself, he disguises himself. Lies and inaccuracy give him a few moments of comfort."[7]

Oddly enough, for a few hours a day I shed my current age for an eighteen-year old, and once again become a young, passionate desirable woman determined to find true love. I hope that you won't judge me too harshly for my confession. I am taking you down a road to make a point regarding Erik so you can recognize the world of illusion he built around his own life to kill the pain.

What were those illusions? His mask, for one, was an illusion. He designed and molded a mask that would hide his appearance and make him look like anyone else. He designed and created a home underneath the opera house, another illusion of a normal life. He dressed a wax figure of Christine in a wedding dress, creating an illusion of Christine being his wife. Ultimately, his world of illusion led him down a road of obsession.

The Phantom not only used illusion for comfort, but he used illusion to control others. The entire opera house was an illusion, filled with secret passageways and trapdoors to catch the unsuspecting, which he helped design and built for his own use.

So what is an illusion? If you need a cold hard dictionary definition, it is something that deceives. Illusion produces a false or misleading impression of reality. You may not believe that your own life is influenced by illusion, but I assure you every day you participate in it some way. Every time you watch a movie, read a book, wish you could fall in love with the Phantom or become Christine, you leave reality and cross into illusion.

Why do we do it? Creating an illusion through storytelling is nothing new. It has been around for centuries as a tool humans use to cope. Reality can be harsh, life cruel, living in our world hectic and draining. We find ways to compensate and comfort ourselves. We often find characters we can identify with and hold onto them deluding ourselves in an illusion we are like them, or as in roleplaying, we live vicariously through the character. Again, buried in *The Phantom of the Opera*, and embodied in Erik, is another interesting facet of our humanity. He is quite complex using illusion and myth to find comfort in his life.

Remember too, the story is an illusion, a character created in the mind of Gaston Leroux, a writer. I know many fans believe Erik was a real man, and I am not here to argue that point or dispel anyone's beliefs or offend anyone by my next statement. However, I find it interesting that Gaston Leroux lived during the Victorian age when magicians and illusionists were enjoying a golden age of their own. It makes me wonder how much of an illusion he wove into the book and his statements that Erik truly lived underneath the Paris Opera House. What do you think? Is his story illusion or truth?

(POSTED SUNDAY, JUNE 8, 2008)

Lair

"Erik . . . guarding the approaches to his lair."
Gaston Leroux

In case you do not realize it, I love *The Phantom of the Opera*. When I think that I have squeezed every living morsel out of the story, some life experience or inspiration hits me between the eyes and another part screams symbolism.

When it came to writing a post regarding the lair, I put it on the shelf for a long time. Frankly, I did not know what to write and found myself stuck in a bad case of writer's block. It has taken me forty-two posts on my blog to find an application to its existence, but I believe it will touch your heart.

What is the Phantom's lair? What does it symbolize? Well, it's obviously his home, hideout, den, hangout, retreat, and hideaway (love the Thesaurus). You will notice his lair is surrounded by the boundary of a lake to keep you from the inner sanctum of his world. For me, his lair symbolizes his inner heart, and the lake the boundary set to protect himself from the cruelties of the world outside. Let me explain the analogy.

Boundaries serve the purpose of protection from intruders. A boundary can be a fence, brick wall, or a moat as a symbol to others—do not cross this line. The Phantom does not want you to enter his lair. For extra assurance, he has those tricky trapdoors everywhere, and just in case someone traverses the lake and makes it across, he seals the entrance with a gate. The lair is a haven. It is that one solitary location where he feels safe.

No one from the outside world can stand before him and call him ugly because of his deformity. There is no one at the shore pointing fingers and laughing at his mask. There are no voices of condemnation ridiculing him while he composes "Don Juan Triumphant." There are no crude remarks thrown his way like daggers passing by candlesticks burning him with hot wax. He has pulled the gate down at the entrance and locked everyone out. He makes a conscious decision not to expose his heart to the lack of compassion and mean cruelty of the world outside.

So what is this behavior? Is he a loner that lacks social skills that will not let you in? Remember, the Phantom seeks redemption and yearns for acceptance and love. Believe it or not, he has the right to protect himself from what he allows in his lair and is wise to do so.

Setting limits around our heart is what psychologists define as erecting boundaries. Boundaries define where you end and someone else begins. This is you; this is me. Our personal lair is the inner soul and heart of who we are as individuals. It is a place beyond the lake you do not wish others to cross. It does not mean no one can ever enter. If I choose, I can send you the gondola and a paddle to cross the lake. Nevertheless, if you dare to come uninvited, do not be surprised if I stand on the shore and yell to get out! Can you hear the anger of the Phantom when someone crosses his boundaries into his lair uninvited, *"How dare you enter!"* Why? It is because he feels threatened.

We control our own boundaries, and we choose who or what can cross that line. The Phantom did so with Christine. He trusted and allowed her to cross the boundary into his inner world. There is a risk, however, in letting others into our lair. Some people are safe, but some are not.

In reality, each of us needs a safe space. Having healthy boundaries in relationships is a means of protecting our hearts and souls from those who would enter and hurt us. A wise king once wrote:

"Above all else, guard your heart, for it is the wellspring of life." (Proverbs 4:23)

If we do not watch over our heart, we put ourselves at risk. People who never learn to set healthy boundaries in relationships suffer throughout their lifetime needlessly.

I learned the meaning of boundaries some years ago through purchasing a wonderful book, which was a lifesaver. Because I lived so many years without boundaries, it took a long time for me to dig a trench around my lair and surround myself with a lake. It also made people close to me angry that I was under construction and attempting to change the playing field. In the past,

I let them invade my territory, and now I was telling them to keep out.

I am happy to report that construction is complete, and I stand and look across at the shore and ponder who is asking for admittance to my lair. I may look at one and say, okay, that person is safe. I will send the gondola over to you. Then I will see another and say, there is no way in hell I am giving that person a paddle! I leave them on the shore, turn away, close the gate, and stay safe knowing I am keeping a boundary protecting my heart.

Is it far-fetched symbolism? Perhaps, or maybe it really hits home. Do you feel like there is no lake dug around your liar? Have you dug your trench? I have shovels if you need them and will help you fill the lake with water.

My lake I filled with tears.

(POSTED THURSDAY, DECEMBER 11, 2008)

Masquerade

*"Very well, you shall see that tonight.
Come to the masked ball."*
Gaston Leroux

The history of the masquerade is quite fascinating. The event originated in Venice Italy in the fifteenth century as elaborate dances for the upper class, which eventually evolved into costumed balls and festivals for the public. The masquerade spread in popularity throughout Europe in the seventeenth and eighteenth century, which was an event that brought people together of all classes, both noblemen and commoners. It became an outlet for many to depart from their lives and enter into the world of pretend, hiding themselves behind masks and costumes and taking on another identity.

The most frequently used masquerade costume was the domino, which was a very simple disguise consisting of a black loose hooded cloak covering the body accompanied by a mask either white or black in color. It gave the illusion of intrigue and mystery.

The Phantom's disguise was similar to the

domino. His head is concealed by a wig, his face hidden by a mask, his body enveloped in a cloak of black. It provides him the opportunity to hide his hideous appearance and become someone who was mysterious, alluring, seductive, and attractive. Of course, he arrives at the masquerade dressed as Red Death, which I discuss at length in another article.

Even today in the twenty-first century, there are costume parties and masquerade balls where you can take on another identity and hide the real you behind a costume. Often unsatisfied with our own identity in real life, being part of a masquerade provides an opportunity to become another more mysterious, alluring, and seductive in appearance. I would imagine though, just like the mask, we could wear emotional costumes to hide behind as well.

If we had a masquerade ball at the opera house, what costume would you choose? Your choices are the characters in *The Phantom of the Opera*. As for me, I would become Meg Giry, curious about who was Christine's great tutor.

(POSTED THURSDAY, JANUARY 31, 2008)

Opera!

"Erik was one of the chief contractors under Philippe Garnier, the architect of the Opera . . . "
Gaston Leroux

Opera! After all, it is the Opera Ghost's favorite form of entertainment, and it is the setting for the story *The Phantom of the Opera*. So what is all the hype in Paris about opera anyway in the mid-nineteenth century? Plenty!

During that time period, numerous composers, French, Italian, and others throughout Europe, wrote several famous operas. Paris in the nineteenth century had two opera houses. The original opera house was called the Théâtre de l'Académie Royale de Musique, which was destroyed by a massive fire. It had been the chief opera house in Paris and center for ballet since opening in 1821.

The second opera house in Paris, built by Garnier, opened in 1875. Of course, the Opera Populaire is a fictional name given by Andrew Lloyd Webber.

Grand Opera in the nineteenth century usually contained four or five acts and were lavish productions with large casts, orchestras, outstanding designs, and sets. Ballet at the Opera originated in Paris, and ballet performances usually appeared near the beginning of the second act as part of the performance to satisfy the wealthy aristocrats who enjoyed the ballet dancers. Do you see any correlation there between Comte Philippe de Chagny and his interest in the ballerina La Sorelli that Leroux mentions? It was common for rich patrons to receive special favors from the ballerinas backstage if you get my drift.

Attending operas was an important aspect of social life. While doing research for one of my books, I came across an interesting historical comment for wealthy men:

"It is imperative for a man of fashion to appear at the opera on Friday's."

Let's look at the operas performed or mentioned in *The Phantom of the Opera*. Are they real operas or the imagination of Leroux and Webber?

The first opera mentioned in Webber's work is at auction with Lot 663, the production poster of *Hannibal* by Chalumeau. This is a fictional work though there is an opera by the name of "*Hannibal.*"

The second mentioned in Webber's work at auction was Lot 664, "a wooden pistol and three human skulls, from the production of '*Robert le Diable*' by Meyerbeer." Boy, talk about symbolism in that reference! This was an opera written by Giacoma Meyerbeer. *Robert le Diable* translated means "Robert the Devil."

The third opera in Webber's work, *Il Muto*, is

a fictional work in the story, as well as *Don Juan Triumphant*, of course, written by the Phantom.

The opera Leroux mentions in his work, *Faust*, is an opera about making a pack with the Devil. There are also numerous other works mentioned in Leroux's version, which are actual works and composers:

"All the great composers of the day had conducted their own works in turns. Faure and Krauss had sung; and, on that evening, Christine Daaé had revealed her true self, for the first time, to the astonished and enthusiastic audience. Gounod had conducted the Funeral March of a Marionnette; Reyer, his beautiful overture to Siguar; Saint Saens, the Danse Macabre and a Reverie Orientale; Massenet, an unpublished Hungarian march; Guiraud, his Carnaval; Delibes, the Valse Lente from Sylvia and the Pizzicati from Coppelia. Mlle. Krauss had sung the bolero in the Vespri Siciliani; and Mlle. Denise Bloch the drinking song in Lucrezia Borgia. But the real triumph was reserved for Christine Daaé, who had begun by singing a few passages from Romeo and Juliet..." (by Gounod).

To truly understand and appreciate any story, knowing the history of the items mentioned in the work enhances it even more.

Opera anyone?

(POSTED SATURDAY, OCTOBER 11, 2008)

Section Five
Thoughts from Gaston Leroux

Heaven or Hell
Hideous Lies
Horror
Intimidation
Morality
Poor Unhappy Erik
Skeleton, Skulls, and Roses

Heaven or Hell

"No, he is not a ghost; he is a man of Heaven and earth, that is all."
Gaston Leroux

Leroux weaves a tale in *The Phantom of the Opera* that is filled with essential elements. Religion is one dominant theme, which Webber certainly carries on in the stage play. As I mentioned before, the story itself and lyrics by Charles Hart are riddled with scriptural references.

Everyone in the story has a belief system of one type or another. Heaven, hell, and superstition are everywhere. Let's take a quick look at heaven and hell in *The Phantom of the Opera* and the belief systems that influenced the characters' behaviors.

France during the time of 1870 just entered into the Third Republic, and Catholicism was the state religion though there were Protestants and Jews in France as well. Raoul makes a statement while being interviewed by the public prosecutor, that he is Catholic. In fact, he's a bit insulted when the prosecutor asks if he's superstitious!

"Are you superstitious? No Monsieur, I am a

practicing Catholic!"

Why the obvious horror at the question? Those who were educated and rich characterized the superstitious as feeble-minded individuals. No wonder Raoul is appalled at the prosecutor's question, which is a blatant insult to his class and title as Vicomte.

Was Christine Catholic? Probably not. Remember she came from Sweden, and during that time period the Church of Sweden, which is a branch of Lutheran Christianity, was the state religion. Leroux writes that Gustav Daaé was, "*a peasant who lived there with his family, digging the earth during the week and singing in the choir on Sundays*," which leads me to believe she was Protestant.

I find it quite interesting that Raoul wonders about Christine's belief system commenting on Madame Valerius' influence of a simple-minded woman and her dead father who he calls a "superstitious fiddler," perhaps referring to her Protestant roots. Raoul thinks they are foolish to believe in the Angel of Music, who comes down from Heaven to haunt the dressing rooms of the Opera.

The theatrical characters are riddled with fear and driven by superstition. As I researched this article, I found some interesting historical references to various theatrical superstitions and especially those involving opera.

Leroux states that Sorelli was very superstitious, as well as Gabriel. Theatrical residents were clearly influenced by superstitious fears of ghosts, demons, saints, and angels that resided in their world at the opera house. No wonder that having a resident Opera Ghost was such a big deal.

What about Erik? He seems to use religion and superstition to his advantage. Here's an interesting statement about using superstition as a means of control:

"Poligny was superstitious and Erik knew it. Erik knew most things about the public and private affairs of the Opera. When M. Poligny heard a mysterious voice tell him, in Box Five, of the manner in which he used to spend his time and abuse his partner's confidence, he did not wait to hear any more. Thinking at first that it was a voice from Heaven, he believed himself damned..."

Erik was also a master at using scripture and religious tones to entice and mesmerize Christine. He plays upon her weakness in believing in the Angel of Music. Christine confesses his influence in the following:

"And then the voice began to sing the leading phrase, 'Come! And believe in me! Whoso believes in me shall live! Walk! Whoso hath believed in me shall never die! I cannot tell you the effect which that music had upon me. It seemed to command me, personally, to come, to stand up and come to it."

What about Erik's personal beliefs? Well, clearly he thought himself damned, an Angel of Hell, rather than of Heaven, for which there was no redemption.

What religious terms did Christine use to describe him? She goes from heaven to hell.

"No, he is not a ghost; he is a man of Heaven and Earth, that is all."

"He is a demon!"

Then, of course, the references continue from Raoul, the Persian, and everyone else that Erik is akin to the Devil and looks like Satan himself with death's head.

Religion in our lives and our belief systems are a very personal matter. However, it's very obvious in Leroux's work, as well as Webber, religion and superstition are influencing all the key players. *The Phantom of the Opera* is a story of light and darkness, heaven and hell, love and hate, redemption and damnation. Each person's belief in their own personal way reflects their actions and emotions throughout the story, from Raoul being a practicing Catholic, the simple-minded beliefs of Christine, to the superstitions of the cast. Religion for some of the characters is a guiding light or for others a tool of manipulation. It can comfort the heart at the thought of heaven, or bring terror to the soul at the thought of hell.

Each of us possesses some type of personal belief system, and it's those beliefs that guide our lives, morals, and actions in everyday life. You may be deeply religious, a non-believer, or the superstitious type. Even if you believe in nothing, you still believe in something!

(POSTED SATURDAY, JULY 18, 2009)

Horror

"He fills me with horror and I do not hate him."
Gaston Leroux

As I focus on Leroux, one element I haven't talked about before is horror. *Le Fantôme de l'Opéra* falls within the genre of Gothic literature, which inherently includes the elements of both horror and romance combined together.

Leroux's book is filled with instances of extreme emotion, fearfulness, ghosts, dark cellars, danger, death, decay, disfigurement, and a madman the Persian calls a monster. On top of that, we have elements of kidnapping, captivity, bondage, torture, strangulation, and death.

The setting is dark and mysterious. A ghost lives in the cellars underneath the Opera House and sleeps in a coffin. The path to his lair is filled with dark, creepy corridors, dangerous trapdoors, and an ominous lake that takes lives.

Leroux weaves symbolism throughout the book touching on the darker side. There are references to hell, damnation, graveyards, and the Devil. Even another horror writer, Edgar Allen Poe's work, *Red Death*, is woven into the story. I'm sure if you look hard enough, you can find many more symbols of horror throughout with the intent to frighten the reader.

As I write this post, I'm back to my curiosity of human behavior. You know, I've termed *The Phantom of the Opera* my psychological playground, and this is definitely one that takes me to the sandbox.

So what is it about the genre of horror fiction that attracts us for entertainment purposes? We love to watch aliens invade earth, vampires sucking blood out of necks, monsters on rampages, and ugly men capture beautiful girls dragging them to their lair. Theaters entertain people with thrills of chainsaw massacres and humans eating humans. Gothic novels about the darker side of horror and romance are big business, as well as films that dabble on the dark side.

Perhaps it's the adrenaline rush we get having the daylights scared out of us or it is true that human nature loves darkness rather than light. I'm sure, unless you're a little psycho yourself, you really wouldn't wish to be on the receiving end of some of these horrific acts. Frankly, I don't think I would have liked being kidnaped and dragged down to the Opera House cellars and bound by a disfigured madman who could blow me to smithereens.

As for Gothic literature, it appears we like to throw in the element of romance to smooth the rough edges of horror itself. The character gives succumbs to the darker side and falls in love with the creepy guy with a mask or the blood sucking vampire. Somehow, I guess that makes it better and appeals to those women who love those bad-boys or their captors.

Whatever the reason, *The Phantom of the Opera* is a classic Gothic romance and horror literature. It contains all the elements of fright and love mixed together.

(POSTED SUNDAY, AUGUST 16, 2009)

Intimidation

"Take my advice and be warned in time. O. G."
Gaston Leroux

Writing strictly about Leroux is interesting. While examining Andrew Lloyd Webber's version, sprinkled with Leroux as a backdrop, the story is more romanticized. However, with Leroux alone, without the Webber content, I find the story dramatically taking on a different form in a myriad of ways—especially when it comes to some of the darker sides of Erik.

He is a master of many things, and one of his tools to get his way in life is through intimidation, which he uses as a means of control. He can be polite as the next person, as long as you do his bidding, but wrathful as hell if you dare to do otherwise. Consider the following:

(1) he's territorial
(2) he demands obedience
(3) he declares war should you dare ignore his commands
(4) he uses intimidation and threats to get his way, and
(5) he ultimately punishes you for daring to

defy him.

His first threat arrives as he insists on maintaining his territorial rights. The managers must learn his ways, and he threatens through that conditional little word of "if."

"*If you wish to live in peace, you must not begin by taking away my private box.*"

Secondly, he manipulates obedience through ultimatums. I call it emotional blackmail. You must do this or I'll do that.

"*If you still care for peace, here is my ultimatum. It consists of the four following conditions...*"

His conditions, of course, overflow with musts and wills.

"*You must...*"
"*I will...*"
"*Shall be...*"
"*I absolutely insist...*"
"*You will...*"

Thirdly, he intimidates you by giving dire warnings to instill fear as a means of control.

"*Take my advice and be warned in time.*"

Finally, the threat of impending doom arrives should you dare to disobey.

"*If you refuse, you will give FAUST tonight in a house with a curse upon it.*"

I do find it quite amusing that he signs his name, "*Your Most Humble and Obedient Servant, OPERA GHOST.*" Yes, humbly yours, as long as you stay on his good side.

Well, it's obvious that our Ghost has some personality issues. What are they? Intimidation is not a new tactic by any means. Basically, it's instilling fear in another to control their will either by coercion or threats. You can call it skillful manipulation. We usually intimidate people to dominate and control as O.G. did. The new managers threatened his domination, and his only means of keeping it was by intimidation. It's a means to an end, whether we do it consciously or subconsciously. However, those on the receiving end might not necessarily like it. The managers were a bit peeved.

"'*Look here, I'm getting sick of him, sick of him!' shouted Richard, bringing his fists down on his office table.*"

Those who use intimidation as a means of control eventually find out if their tactics are successful or not. If the person at the receiving end is weak, dependent, easily preyed upon, prone to fear, and has low self-esteem, it's success indeed. However, if they find someone who doesn't respond to their intimidation and threats, it usually ends up in a war of wits. Believe me, no one wins.

I've always used this powerful analogy in some ways. Negative things in our lives can be likened to a weed—unwanted, distressful, or a nuisance. The trouble with weeds, as you know, is if you continue to water them, they grow and deepen their roots. When you try to pull the dang thing out, it's a struggle to get it out of the ground, if not impossible. Usually when you do pull it out, the weed grows back again because the root system is still intact.

It's the same with those who use the Opera Ghost's masterful techniques. If their tactics work, and people respond to demands, it gives great satisfaction to the controller. It feeds their need to continue to control. The recipient of intimidation folds, obeys their demands, is filled with distress, and surrenders out of fear.

On the other hand, psychologists suggest not to respond or address the demands of a controlling person. It feeds the weed, makes it stronger, and gives back the craving attention to the controller. Just like anything else, when you fail to feed something, it will shrivel up at the roots and die.

There are some great articles on the Internet on psychology sites on how to deal with individuals that have controlling personalities. Take the time to check them out if you feel like a victim of intimidation. You'll be a stronger person in the end.

(POSTED FRIDAY, JUNE 19, 2009)

Lies

"What more can I tell you, dear? You now know the tragedy. It went on for a fortnight—a fortnight during which I lied to him. My lies were as hideous as the monster who inspired them; but they were the price of my liberty."
Gaston Leroux

Reading Leroux once again is an inspiration. Just this morning a few statements made by Raoul and Christine flew off the pages revealing topics and character motivations that I have not touched on before. Christine's statement above was certainly one of them. *Lies*

If you have not studied the original novel, Leroux will shock some of the die-hard fans of Webber's portrayal of the story. I've used quite a bit of Leroux's written work to expound on the motivations of the characters we see in Webber's version, but there are other aspects of the story that might surprise you. Christine's lies to the hideous monster might be one of them.

Christine is a very complex woman, to say the least, and so is her relationship with Erik. How she interacts with him throughout the original book is one bipolar experience to put it mildly. She thinks him a supernatural being, an angel from heaven and then discovers he's not an angel, but a man. She admires his genius, is horrified by his appearance, fears his actions, and declares to Raoul she does not hate him and that he fills her with horror. Christine confesses that horror was the motivation behind her lies to Erik to buy her liberty.

It's interesting that only in a few chapters earlier, Leroux pens these words when Christine answers a question from Raoul, *"She was incapable of lying."* Was she incapable of lying to Raoul, but capable of lying to Erik; or did she lie to Raoul that she lied to Erik? Now I have your head spinning.

Whatever the reason behind her lies, we can conclude that any lying is birthed from some motivation, or the deceit would never fall from our lips. I can think of five reasons, and no doubt you can think of more.

We lie to protect ourselves as Christine did in the situation with Erik. She feared for her life, so she lied to find favor.

We lie to protect others so they won't get hurt by some truth we feel would be detrimental.

We lie with the intent to deceive others for our gain.

We lie to cover our actions. It started with Cain and Abel, *"Where is Abel your brother?"* asks God. "*I do not know*," responds Cain. Oh, sure, you just killed the dude. Liar.

We lie because we are just habitual liars, which is an evil inclination. The Devil is the liar of them all, *". . . for he is a liar and the father of lies."* (John 8:44)

Well, we've all been lied to, and we've probably all told lies either big or small. The resultant outcome of those lies can vary in our lives. I know I've been devastated by lies told to me by people I've trusted. So why do we do it? How come we just can't come out with it! If the truth sets us free, why do we bind ourselves in lies? An interesting analogy that Christine felt her freedom would come from lies instead of truth.

There are multiple inferences of lying throughout the story. So whom do we believe? Wait! There's another post coming down the line as to what the characters believed to be truth, but in the meantime I leave you with this quote to ponder:

"A lie told often enough becomes the truth." (Lenin)

(POSTED SATURDAY, MAY 16, 2009)

Morality

"Is Christine still a good girl?"
Gaston Leroux

I have been doing research lately on the life of Gaston Leroux, who is responsible for all this Phantom Obsession Compulsive Disorder in the world (my new coined phrase of POCD).

Leroux was quite the colorful man, who led a rather wild life. Various biographies are filled with all sorts of interesting tidbits. He inherited a million francs upon his father's death and afterward acquired a taste for alcohol and gambling. Subsequently, he pilfered his fortune away in casinos. After much of it was gone, he turned to work as a theater critic and reporter and eventually became a full-time journalist to make a living.

As far as his personal love life, he married his first wife and soon afterward was involved in an affair with another woman who became his mistress. He sired two children with her out of wedlock, and then finally when his first wife agreed to grant him a divorce years later, he married his lover. He struggled with a gambling problem throughout his lifetime and died with very little money in spite of his success. Another interesting and detailed biography states that Leroux had a darker side that fixated on horror, fantasy, and aspects of macabre.

I'm not sure if I hear many gasps over that revelation of Leroux's lifestyle, but it's an important introduction to this post on morality in *The Phantom of the Opera*. What we've glorified in the story of the redemption of the Opera Ghost, was written by a man who clearly wasn't a saint. This post is not to judge his morality by any means, except to say that much of how he lived during that time period in France was frankly just a way of life.

If you look closely at the original, you'll see the subject of morality and the Parisian lifestyle sprinkled throughout the story. Unless you're familiar with the times and practices, some of the innuendos may not be that noticeable to you. The reality of how things really were in Parisian society among the Opera patrons, ballerinas, and divas, is frankly "R-rated." It's not the "PG" romance we've come to idolize.

Those cute little ladies in the tutus known as the corps de ballet or ballet rats were young girls who trained and performed as ballerinas. Most of them came from poor, working-class families. Degas, a French artist of that era, painted many pictures of the ballerinas who danced upon the stage. A good article to read is "Degas and His Dancers" by Paul Trachtman (you can find it on the Internet) that discusses how getting backstage was a privilege paid for by wealthy male subscription holders, called abonnés, who flirted with the dancers.

At the time *The Phantom of the Opera* was set, ballerinas were considered to be the "echelon of prostitution." Prostitution in France was legal, and married men often had mistresses and enjoyed sexual pleasures away from their marriage beds.

If you read Leroux closely early in the story, it's mentioned that Comte Philippe de Chagny would not have taken his brother behind the scenes of the Opera, but Raoul had asked him insistently to do so. Philippe knew morality backstage was loose. It mentions later that he had planned when Raoul returned from the Navy to introduce him to the life behind the curtains. When Raoul goes backstage to check on Christine's welfare after she faints, Philippe is surprised that Raoul already knows the way to her dressing room. In this scene and in many others the subscribers are crowding around the ballerinas.

The story goes on to express Philippe's displeasure over Raoul wishing to marry Christine. After all, those in her profession were of the lower class. They were fine for flirtation and sexual pleasures but not meant for marriage. It would have been scandalous for Raoul to marry beneath his status, but as you know, he defied his elder brother in the matter and it led to much contention between the two of them.

Gaston Leroux writes that Philippe de Chagny had an "understanding" with Sorelli, the prima ballerina. Philippe spent his time backstage as quite the bachelor himself, and it's obvious by

Leroux's inference that Sorelli was Philippe's mistress. In fact, he says in defense of the Comte's actions:

"But it could hardly be reckoned as a crime for this nobleman, a bachelor, with plenty of leisure, especially since his sisters were settled, to come and spend an hour or two after dinner in the company of a dancer."

What about the divas? That's another interesting study in itself too, where you will find famous divas of the past who were wealthy courtesans of aristocrats during their careers. I think this possibility played upon Raoul's fears regarding Christine. At one point, he questions Madame Valerius on whether Christine is, *"still a good girl"* after he learns of her going away with her mysterious genius. It's apparent the question of Christine's morality came quickly to Raoul's mind based on her behavior, and he still wasn't convinced after Madame Valerius had said she was still a good girl.

"He walked home to his brother's house in a pitiful state. He could have struck himself, banged his head against the walls! To think that he had believed in her innocence, in her purity!"

It's almost comical how upset Raoul becomes, as he pours his heart out to his brother. Philippe tells him Christine had been spotted the night before in a carriage with another man, and Raoul believes it to be her lover. To bury his pain, Leroux writes:

"Raoul dressed in frantic haste, prepared to forget his distress by flinging himself, as people say, into 'the vortex of pleasure.'"

I think we all know what pleasures are alluded to here. However, poor Raoul never makes it that far.

Of course, Andrew Lloyd Webber's original stage version of *The Phantom of the Opera* strips all the nasty reality away, as we see portrayed a more innocent version of its characters and time. We love the cute Meg Giry and ballerinas in their tutus flitting about the stage, the innocent and young Christine, and handsome Raoul. The only sexual reference made is the "*pleasures of the flesh*" that the Phantom has been denied in life. Of course, there is a rather passionate scene in the lair during "The Music of the Night," as he entices Christine into his world. The "Point of No Return," is filled with desire.

In stark contrast, we come to the sequel, *Love Never Dies*, which strips away the fantasy and portrays a more accurate version of morality of its day, with fallen characters who drink, gamble, and have sex out of wedlock that results in an illegitimate child. It's the unpleasant storyline some fans dislike, and then others are not so appalled because they understand that humanity is often filled with broken and imperfect humans who make mistakes.

When we study life during the late nineteenth century in Paris, where the story is set, it helps us part the curtain between reality and romantic fantasy. Even Gaston Leroux, the very author himself, struggled with his own vices of drinking, gambling, illicit affairs, and illegitimate children. In the day and age when *The Phantom of the Opera* was first released in France, the public readers no doubt understood his innuendos regarding morality between its pages.

In closing, I can't help but ask myself one question in light of Leroux's own lifestyle. Would he relate to the recent sequel adaptation of the story or would he be offended? It's an honest question to ponder, but one I think most would rather not think about in light of the similarities.

(POSTED SATURDAY, OCTOBER 9, 2010)

Poor Unhappy Erik

> *"Poor, unhappy Erik! Shall we pity him? Shall we curse him? He asked only to be some one, like everybody else. But he was too ugly! And he had to hide his genius . . . when, with an ordinary face, he would have been one of the most distinguished of mankind!"*
> Gaston Leroux

The above quote from the original novel poses two questions to its readers regarding Erik. After you've read the story, Monsieur Leroux asks how you feel about the Opera Ghost. Shall we pity him? Shall we curse him? His next statement is a profound truth of mankind that Erik was deemed unworthy because he was too ugly. He was a genius in his own right but was forced to hide because he did not possess an ordinary face. Society would not accept him based on his outward appearance, and hence his talented gifts never distinguished him with mankind.

It's no secret that beauty is revered and rewarded, and ugliness is disdained and shunned. We judge abilities, worth, and talents by the outward appearance of a man, rather than the inward gifts they may possess. If talented gifts are not wrapped in a visually appealing package, we rarely pay any attention.

I love beauty just as much as the next person, and I often wonder when we look at another person what makes them attractive to us or not? Why does our brain distinguish between beauty and ugliness?

Long ago when the *Twilight Zone* was a big hit on TV (boy that dates me), I distinctly remember one episode where the tables were turned. All the ugly people were deemed beautiful, and all the beautiful people were deemed ugly, and as a result they suffered prejudice in society due to their appearance.

So the question still stands? Shall we pity him? Shall we curse him? When you see a deformed person, do you pity them for their lot in life or do you turn away in disgust because of their ugliness? Remember once again that the true value of beauty is determined by what's in our heart. One can be beautiful on the outside, and truly ugly on the inside.

(POSTED FRIDAY, MAY 8, 2009)

Skeletons, Skulls & Roses

"They were marvelous red roses that had blossomed in the morning, in the snow, giving a glimpse of life among the dead, for death was all around him."
Gaston Leroux

I am starting this post with a warning: this is going to be a morbid subject. Don't blame me! It's Leroux's fault. He's the one who wove this theme into the story, and it's the subject most of us avoid—death. He penned the word often enough to make you face it at the turn of nearly every page. He uses the word death seventy-nine times and dead forty-nine. Is he trying to make a point here or just use scare tactics for a horror story? The subject is not only forced upon its readers, it's forced upon its characters. Let's look and see how they perceive death's door.

In my first set of posts, I talk about Christine's walk through the graveyard. It's obvious Christine's experience with death encompasses one overwhelming element of grief. Her life profoundly changes by the death of her father. In fact so much, Leroux writes that she lost with him, her voice, her soul, and her genius. She struggles throughout the story mourning her father's passing.

Raoul, on the other hand, has his own graveyard experience. His encounter with death revolves around another element of fear. His close encounter with the Ghost in the graveyard scares the daylights out of him. Skulls roll at his feet, he follows a cloaked figure, touches his hem, sees what he describes as the face of Satan, and passes out. Later in the story, he is faced with death again and finds himself in the torture chamber of mirrors about to go insane from fear.

Leroux also weaves into the story another element. We have two characters who, unfortunately, taste death for themselves—Joseph Buquet and Philippe de Chagny. Of course, there are numerous references to others who die at the hand of Erik either through strangulation or his trapdoors and torture chamber.

The Persian, on the other hand, avoids it at all cost. He knows Erik is capable of inflicting death. He worries about others and warns them that death could be waiting should they encounter Erik and his trapdoors and torture chamber. He's careful, and he uses caution so he doesn't meet death before his time.

Finally, we have Erik. I can think of one description when it comes to death. He embraces it. Death is everywhere in his persona as the Opera Ghost. He calls himself Red Death Stalking Abroad and is constantly referred to as possessing death's head. To top it off, his bedroom looks like a funeral parlor, and he sleeps inside a coffin! As I stated in my earlier post on Red Death, I believe Erik thought that death was the one place of equality he found with the rest of humanity.

Curiously though, Leroux doesn't leave us in the midst of death without weaving another theme throughout. It's how we deal with death; hence the inspiration for my title, "*Skeletons, Skulls, and Roses*." The following paragraph tells it all.

"*Raoul walked away, dejectedly, to the graveyard in which the church stood and was indeed alone among the tombs, reading the inscriptions; but, when he turned behind the apse, he was suddenly struck by the dazzling note of the flowers that straggled over the white ground. They were marvelous red roses that had blossomed in the morning, in the snow, giving a glimpse of life among the dead, for death was all around him . . . Skeletons and skulls by the hundred were heaped against the wall of the church . . .*"

Leroux attempts to bring reprieve about all this talk of death through the use of flowers. There are roses in the graveyard for Raoul to glimpse life among the dead. Madame Giry tells the managers the Opera Ghost leaves roses behind in his box for her to discover. Christine states Erik's drawing room is decorated and furnished with nothing but flowers.

When you think of it, we do leave life among the dead. Funeral homes are filled with flowers during services, and traditionally we leave flowers when visiting a grave. Even Erik in the movie version leaves a glimpse of life on Christine's grave, a red rose. Perhaps flowers are not for the dead but for us who are left behind. They bring a sense of comfort and life in the midst of death.

Yes, I know, it's a morbid post, but it's Leroux.

He's the one poking at you this time to face the inevitable, not me. Death is an underlying theme throughout the story Leroux does not wish you to escape.

As a post note, you might be interested in knowing a little about French burial practices in the nineteenth century. Leroux writes, *". . . skeletons and skulls by the hundred were heaped against the wall of the church . . ."*

In my research regarding death for my fiction novel, I discovered the following. The extremely poor, who could not afford a burial plot, were buried in unmarked common graves, which could contain more than one body. Those who could afford to purchase a burial plot had two choices— a temporary plot or one in perpetuity. A temporary plot allowed you a place to rest for five years, and then afterward your body was exhumed and your bones were piled high with others like this churchyard scene. If you lived in Paris, your bones were placed in the catacombs beneath the city. If you were rich, you could buy a plot in perpetuity, which meant you wouldn't be dug up and discarded. You would rest in peace in a crypt or plot marked with a tombstone.

(POSTED WEDNESDAY, JUNE 3, 2009)

Section Six
Love Never Dies

Prologue
The Phantom
Christine Daaé
Raoul, Vicomte de Chagny
Madame Giry
Meg Giry
Gustav

Prologue

Earlier editions of *Lessons From the Phantom of the Opera* purposely omitted any references to *Love Never Dies*, which is Andrew Lloyd Webber's staged sequel. After much thought, I decided to include the following blog posts in this third edition based on the fact that *Love Never Dies* will tour the United States during the 2017-18 season.

I'm not here to debate the rights or wrongs of the story or to discuss how it could have been written differently or whether it should have been written at all. More than anyone, I'm quite aware of the intense opinions in the Phantom community regarding *Love Never Dies*.

On March 24, 2010, I had the opportunity to see the sequel in London shortly after its first release. (A trip to England had been a lifetime desire of mine, since I'm a huge ancestry buff researching my dead ancestors in the U.K.) The sequel was written by Andrew Lloyd Webber and based loosely upon *The Phantom of Manhattan* written by Frederick Forsyth.

I went back to London the following year for more sightseeing and dead ancestor hunting and saw the slightly revised version. The third revised version performed in Melbourne, Sidney, Copenhagen, and Japan, I have only seen on DVD.

The posts in *Lessons From the Phantom of the Opera* regarding the characters are only based on the original 2010-11 version. As far as I can tell, the characters haven't changed—only the staging, costumes, and slight storyline revisions.

My purpose in sharing these posts is to reflect on the story, offer up thoughts, and give you the opportunity to see how these characters have evolved. The end evaluation, may in your eyes, be either good or bad.

Take from my writing whatever you wish, learn lessons if there are any, and find your own interpretation. You might enjoy visiting my blog online to read some of the comments posted by fans regarding the controversies swirling around the sequel, which I think add to a healthy discussion overall.

One final warning, if you are not familiar with the story or the ending, there are spoilers ahead. Proceed with caution.

The Phantom in LND

"Tragedy is a form of art based on human suffering that offers its audience pleasure."
Martin Bahman[8]

The Phantom of the Opera is now Mr. Y. He's a mystery to the public. No longer the Opera Ghost, but a Myster-Y, who no one has seen according to the reporters that greet the de Chagny's at the dock. So who is this man? Well, to look at the present Mr. Y, one must refer back to the Phantom who haunted the Opera Populaire.

I find it very interesting how easily fans accept the Phantom in the first version as a psychopathic murderer who kills without thought, obsesses over a woman, kidnaps her, keeps her in bondage, and blackmails her by threatening to kill Raoul. We easily forgave his transgressions in that version, didn't we? We cheered when Christine showed him the ounce of compassion he so desperately needed and appeared redeemed by love or so we thought. If you haven't read my earlier posts about Erik (His Humanity), Opera Ghost (His Persona), and Phantom (The Spectral Shade), I encourage you to do so in order to remind yourself of the original man behind the mask as you compare the new one now living in New York.

Ten years have past. As most of you realize by now, the story in Webber's musical continued through the song "Beneath the Moonless Sky." Christine returns before her wedding, finds the Phantom, and is sorrowful over her choice. As some of you cringe over the storyline and some have accepted, Christine and the Phantom finally cross that "Point of No Return" they so passionately sung, laced with desire and seduction. It was definitely a moment of no thought of right or wrong, as Christine spoke before, and a child is conceived. As the song further reveals, the Phantom leaves the next morning ashamed of what he has done (or is, as one of my recent commentators interprets) before Christine awakens to swear her love and desire to remain with him.

He runs away to New York, returns to his roots doing freak shows. Finally he builds a life at Coney Island, and we see him ten years later bemoaning his useless existence without Christine. He's depressed, wishes to die, and has no reason to live.

The Phantom has made a new likeness of Christine to replace the one in the lair. The obsession continues. Unable to let go of the past, he's stuck in ancient history but refuses to admit he's got a problem. He's blind to the pain of those around him, self-centered, angry, and a brooding man hell-bent on hearing Christine sing one more time.

The great manipulator is at work again and

woos Christine to New York by offering an enormous amount of money to get what he latter terms "as mine." The master hasn't changed much. He's still short-tempered and insanely driven over his music that now frustrates him because Christine isn't there to sing his creations. His hands still have the tendency to wrap around the throats of others and threaten strangulation throughout the story. Old habits are hard to break.

The Phantom you've grown to love is now a menacing broken-hearted shell of a man carrying an unhealthy obsession over Christine Daaé once again. Sigh. What's wrong with this guy? Didn't he learn a thing in the lair? How come he hasn't grown and changed? Why can't he let the past die and move on? So much for redemption at the kiss of Christine's lips and the culmination of their passions making them one. And to top it off, he really has a warped sense of beauty in his new residence to say the least. Where has it all gone wrong? What must the dude learn to grow into normalcy?

A few key things happen in the story that are turning points to move the Phantom along on the journey he must take. When Christine and the Phantom reunite for the first time, her answer is perhaps not the one he wishes to hear. She declares there is "no now" for either of them and that they must live with their choices. Perhaps at that point he would have accepted it, until another turning point, he discovers that he has a son, Gustav. (Poor Raoul thinks it is his child. Christine has played another betrayal.) The child, however, screams in terror when he sees his father's unmasked face, and once again the Phantom is broken as he realizes not even his own flesh and blood can give him an ounce of compassion.

Like most emotional moments in our lives, he's faced with choices. He decides that he will give anything to his son and at the same time, he relentlessly pursues Christine by making a diabolical bet playing on Raoul's weaknesses. Poor Christine hasn't a clue either. It's that obsessive love returned—what he cannot have willingly, he will take by other means.

What is it going to take to catapult this man into adulthood? Perhaps, he just needs a little more time and the right event to move him along to that end. Let's face it, some of us are a bit more dense when it comes to learning. Is it the pain of our past that shackles us to old behaviors? Does the Phantom after his long existence of pain and rejection deserve just a little more time to put the pieces together? It appears he's going to have to walk through the fire in order to be purified and refined. That's the tragedy of it all that human misery is what often brings us to lasting change.

After all his trickery to gain Christine, she sings for him and Raoul leaves losing the bet. The Phantom knows what has happened and slyly stands quietly as she reads Raoul's departing note—showing no remorse and keeping secret the reason why Raoul has left. He's won the hand.

Well, as you all know, poor Christine is shot by Meg. The Phantom caresses her in his arms and their last kiss happens as life drains from her body. All his desires and obsession have just died in his arms. The woman he has loved his entire life is gone and now all that is left is one thing—a son.

Where does he go from here? A boy once terrified of his father, looks once again upon his face and now shows unconditional love and acceptance. He embraces the beauty underneath—his father. It takes a while before the Phantom is able to embrace his son in return, but finally he does and the curtain comes down.

The story has ended. It's a tragedy indeed that Christine is gone. The two men who fought over her their entire lives have both left empty handed. Did either of them really deserve her?

What now? What do you think happens to the Phantom beyond this point? His obsession lies dead a few feet away. His son has his arms wrapped tightly around his body. Does the man have the capacity to be a father? After all, the Phantom had no father figure and was rejected by his mother. Will being a parent finally teach him sacrificial love? Instead of Christine, perhaps it's really a child of ten that will finally reach the heart of this broken man bringing the final redemption.

Interesting to note the name Gustav means "the staff of gods." Could it be that Gustav is the staff that will lead our dear Phantom to learn the true meaning of sacrificial love? If you've never been a parent, I can tell you it's a role where sacrifice and love consumes your life and never dies!

Do you see anything different now? Formed any new opinions? Has the Phantom really changed in *Love Never Dies* from the original, or is he still a man brought to a point of redemption but by a child this time? Sometimes experience isn't enough to change us—a mere kiss doesn't do the trick—but learning to live and love in action brings lasting change.

My prodding has begun, and I hope you'll see the beauty underneath.

(POSTED THURSDAY, APRIL 1, 2010)

Christine Daae in LND

"The human heart is like a ship on a stormy sea driven about by winds blowing from all four corners of heaven." Martin Luther

This post will probably shock your mask off, because it's going to be the most critical one I have written about the characters in *Love Never Dies*. I've had fun doing my psychological playground thing dissecting each character regarding their personality changes. Christine, however, remains an enigma. As far as I'm concerned, she is by far the most complicated of characters in *The Phantom of the Opera* and *Love Never Dies*.

If I had to use three words to describe Christine in this version, I'd say "twisted every way." I shake my head over this woman's actions in the original and in the sequel. Christine is a product of her childhood in many ways. I see her as a woman who is indecisive, dependent, immature, confused, and torn.

Let's take a look at her actions ten years before her arrival on Coney Island. She was originally torn between two men. She loved the Phantom for his music and passion. She loved Raoul for the security and normal life he could give her. Twisted over her decision, she agrees to betray the Phantom in the end so she can be with Raoul. Then in *Love Never Dies*, we hear she returned to the Phantom and betrayed Raoul! When that doesn't work out as hoped, she returns to Raoul, and betrays him again! And you wonder why the man drinks?

As you know, "Beneath the Moonless Sky" is a song about Christine's indiscretion, if you wish to call it that, in returning to the Phantom before she weds the Vicomte de Chagny. Bad move. She succumbs to the unthinkable, has a one-night stand with the Phantom, and awakens to pledge her love only to find him gone. Rather than seeking him out until she finds him again, she returns to Raoul and proceeds to marry him under the guise she loves him. Does she love Raoul? Does she love the Phantom? Does she love both?

Christine has one big character flaw that her indecision breeds in her—she tends to betray the men she supposedly loves. Instead of being truthful with Raoul before the wedding about her one-night stand and pregnancy (I'm assuming she knew by then), Christine hides the fact and walks down the aisle vowing her love and devotion for Raoul at the altar. What kind of woman does that? What's her motivation? Is Raoul the consolation prize? Is she in love with two men? Okay, of course, this is all just a story.

I suppose if we look deep enough into her motives, we might pity her instead. She's torn between two men that have fought for her affections most of her life. She finds solace now in her son while she's married to a man she really didn't want ten years ago. Did Christine ever make a true choice between the two? I don't think so. In the *Love Never Dies,* she sings for Erik totally unaware of the bet between Raoul and the Phantom. She didn't know the stakes, and she was manipulated again by her Angel and played by Raoul.

Frankly, if you're into tragedy as a solution, the sequel couldn't have ended any other way. Christine had to be taken out of the equation. In her dying breath, she professes again her love for the Phantom, while Raoul returns home defeated and alone.

As much as I love the Phantom story, I really think Christine's decision process is quite twisted in both the original and in the sequel. However, it doesn't take away our obsession over those two star-crossed lovers who can never be together.

(POSTED TUESDAY, MAY 4, 2010)

Raoul, Vicomte de Chagny in LND

"Regret for the things we did can be tempered by time. It is regret for the things we did not do that is inconsolable."
Sydney Smith (1771-1845)

This post will be my third in the line of characters to dissect in *Love Never Dies*. As I continue this journey, I just want to reiterated I'm not here to justify Andrew Lloyd Webber's tinkering of the characters. If you have read my former posts regarding the original characters in *The Phantom of the Opera*, you know that I love to dissect their lives and look into what makes them tick as human beings. What motivations drive them to behave as they do? What lessons, if any, can we learn from their behavior or perhaps relate to in our own lives?

Raoul, in *Love Never Dies*, has changed. Ten years has turned him into a sour apple most of you don't wish to taste. You have taken the first bite, hated the result, and puckered in disgust. Read on. I am merely here to strip off his mask and examine the pain underneath. You may relate—you may not. Whatever you see inside Raoul, Vicomte de

Chagny, just remember by his example, sometimes life turns sour and so do we.

As I did with Meg, let's take a step back and look at Raoul. The same holds true that he is a bit different from Leroux to Webber, but his personality is one we are acquainted with or so we think. What do we know about him? Well, he's a mixture of two stories. He met Christine as a young boy, rescued her scarf that ended up in the sea, went off to the Navy, and came back a man who had traveled the world. He dared to cross the societal lines and pursue a girl beneath his status breaking away from tradition and family to marry.

Webber, however, doesn't go into such depth in his background in the original, but you get the picture. He is the new patron of the Opera House, who sees his childhood sweetheart. The slightly arrogant aristocrat is filled with fanciful romantic intentions, but soon discovers he has a dark rival for Christine's affections. You watch Raoul take a journey from the romantic rooftop under the stars to the bowels of the earth where a noose wraps around his neck. His life hangs in the balance, but he is set free and leaves somewhat changed by the end of the show. He and Christine float off in the gondola and marry. Unfortunately for him, in *Love Never Dies*, Christine has a moonless night with the Phantom that leaves her with a son.

It's now ten years later. He's no longer a young man filled with whimsical romantic ideas. Raoul has grown older and changed. The saint has fallen, and a sinner has emerged. He's irritable, short-tempered, has a gambling habit, and his mistress is alcohol. What happened to Raoul? He was suppose to live happily ever after when he got the girl . . . right?

Raoul is a man struggling with the past. He thought his rival was dead, but unluckily, the Phantom is still haunting him and his wife, as he prophetically spoke in the original play. Why? Because the music is still playing folks! It's the one thing that reminds Raoul of the Phantom. Music is an integral part of what makes Christine. She wants to sing music. Raoul hates her music and says it hurts to hear her sing. Raoul wishes to clip her wings. He want's to silence what she loves. Why? Well, the answer is obvious—it reminds them both of *him*.

Raoul is married to Christine, but he's no fool. He's lived for the past ten years with the realization he cannot give her everything she needs. He only owns half her heart, and no doubt his bruised male ego tells him he's only half a man.

Christine lives with him but raises a son that is not theirs. It's a sad affair of two people together in a half-hearted marriage. Christine finds solace for her emptiness in her son. Raoul on the other hand finds solace by turning to things such as the thrill of gambling and the bottle of alcohol that numbs the pain.

When things couldn't be worse, he's lured to Coney Island and discovers the Phantom is still alive. Once again, he faces his enemy for the affections of his wife. Drunk and reflecting, he wonders why she loves him when all he's given her is sorrow in his attempt to kill the memories of the past. He admits that a different kind of ugliness resides with him—not the outward like the

Phantom possesses but the inward. He talks of wearing his own mask—his outward handsome exterior that hides the shame and despair of his own heart. He faces his demons in a drunken stupor.

Of course, there is more than one demon in Raoul's life, and he arrives to tempt Raoul at his weakest point. They make a bet—two men making a wager to win the heart of one woman. So in a last ditch effort to keep his wife, Raoul swears repentance of his old ways, if she'll just leave and not sing. One must ask though, were his motivations pure or was he truly sorry for how he treated Christine?

We all know lady luck wasn't with him on that bet. Christine sings, and he loses everything. He pens a departing letter filled with regrets for being unable to give her what she really needed and leaves her to the Angel of Music. He is sorrowful, but it's too late. They are no longer the same people. Time, circumstances, and choices have changed them both, and they have drifted apart.

When you take the time to look at each of the characters in *Love Never Dies*, you'll see the theme of regret played in all of them in one degree or the other—the Phantom, Christine, Meg, Madame Giry, and Raoul. I heard it stated long before its release, that *Love Never Dies* is a story of regret and truly that theme is prominent throughout.

In conclusion, what can we take away from examining Raoul's journey? Do you relate to Raoul's pain or not? Do you still see him as just one sour apple of a character? Have you ever drifted apart from a spouse? Have you ever made a choice you regretted? Have you ever looked back on your life and had regrets for how it turned out? Was there a time you sought solace elsewhere in someone or something to kill the pain inside? I think the majority of humanity has dealt with regret. It's how we process it that determines whether we turn into that sour apple or sweet as apple pie.

Raoul is merely human. To compensate for his brokenness, he portrays a rough exterior to mask the pain of a man who couldn't be everything to the woman he loved.

The actors who played the part of Raoul de Chagny in *Love Never Dies* took a controversial role and did a brilliant job portraying the pain of one man who lost everything, giving the audience the capacity to feel sympathy for him rather than loathing.

Also, I find it quite interesting if you read about Gaston Leroux's life that he had a gambling problem and a mistress. The guy was quite colorful, who squandered and drank away his own inheritance. The similarities are a bit stark to say the least.

(POSTED SATURDAY, APRIL 10, 2010)

Madame Giry in LND

"I will complain in the bitterness of my soul."
The Bible

Madame Giry in *Love Never Dies* still dresses in a black dress and wears her black hair in the same tightly coiled bun on top of her head. For this dissection, we will stay focused upon Madame Giry as portrayed in Webber's original stage version and in *Love Never Dies*. To diverge to Leroux or even to the explanations in the movie, will mix the pot far too much. However, I think people will pot mix anyway to draw conclusions or find their own interpretations.

What do we know about Madame Giry from the original Webber version of *The Phantom of the Opera*? Not a whole lot. Where did she come from? Don't know. Who is the father of Meg? Don't know. Why does she like to pound a cane on stage? Don't know. Was she once a proficient ballet performer herself? Don't know. Was she ever married? Don't know. Let's face it, we have very little background in Webber's version. If you need to know more, go talk to Leroux or pen your own conclusions.

What do we know from the original? She cared for Christine as a daughter after her father's death. She delivers the Phantom's notes to everyone. She warns everybody to keep their hands at the level of their eyes. She is the stern ballet mistress to a bunch of giddy little girls. She knows the Phantom tutors Christine and pushes her into the spotlight. She has a daughter she pushes to be a proficient ballet dancer as well.

What does she think of the Phantom? She's proud of who he is and declares his good points— he is a genius, architect, designer, composer, and magician. She warns others of his bad points and tendency to strangle. She's aware the Phantom sees all, knows all, and is capable of dastardly things. She hid him as a child from the cruelties of the world, and over the course of time became a mother figure of sorts to the disfigured lad who grew into manhood underneath the Opera House. She has done his bidding and faithfully served him without complaint.

We know from the story of *Love Never Dies* that she continued to care for him. Like a loving parent, she has gone out of her way to see that he succeeds in his new life, even at the expense of her daughter. (Playing favorites are we?) She hid him again from the world, even after all the dastardly things he had done to Christine and Raoul, along with bringing down the chandelier. The Phantom never had the chance to reap any consequences for his behavior, because Madame Giry rescued him . . . again.

Ten years later, in a fit of frustration over what her pseudo son has become, she lets him have it! He gets a verbal lashing and recap of all her sacrifice on his behalf and tells him he is ungrateful man who can't get his act together. (Gee, sounds to me like a mother and son discussion during turbulent teenage years.)

No use rehashing all the words spoken in that scene of the show. The woman has poured her life out for one man since he was a boy. Let's face it, she's a tad bit frustrated to say the least and probably menopausal too at her age—a lethal combination.

There is a lot going on inside that tightly wound bun upon Madame Giry's head. It appears the coil has finally sprung. She's disappointed in the Phantom. She's bitter because she gave her life and received nothing in return. She's upset because her daughter wants his approval but never receives it. She aging and now everything she had worked for will be given to the Phantom's son. Who will care for her and Meg now? There goes her retirement years!

If we look at Madame Giry a bit closer, you might see that deep down inside she is reacting like a parent with a terribly disappointing child. She is a woman filled with bitterness, because all the love, care, and concern she has poured into the Phantom has not reaped the outcome she hoped.

The question came to mind as I wrote in my original post about Madame Giry that she could be partially to blame for the Phantom's immature development. After all, she hid him from the cruelties of the world and rescued him from reaping consequences in his life more than one time. Do you think she was a good mother to Meg? Chew on that one.

Everyone has a breaking point in life where hurts pile up, disappointments bury us, and bitterness results. Madame Giry has played her own part in this play of characters; and though she blames the Phantom for most of her woes, she is a tad bit guilty for the outcome. Like any psychological playground, there is a wealth of possibilities here to explain her actions in *Love Never Dies*.

What do you think about Madame Giry now? Is she just an old biddy with a bad attitude, another character stuck in a bad plot, or a woman who feels unappreciated, disappointed, and resentful? If you know anything about personality traits, people who are chronic rescuers often end up with those feelings, because they are spent, frustrated, and empty inside. It's the perfect breeding ground for bitterness.

As usual, I've poked, now go think it over and come up with your own interpretation of the angry lady in a black taffeta dress.

(POSTED SATURDAY, APRIL 17, 2010)

Meg Giry in LND

"Those whose approval you seek most give you the least."
Maurice Chevalier

Meg Giry, is the little ballerina from the Opera Populaire. We remember her as the one who held the mask of the Phantom when the curtain came down at the end of the original production. If you've read my posts about Meg beforehand, you already know that Leroux and Webber portray her differently.

Since we're looking at Meg from *Love Never Dies*, let's focus on this version and see what's happened the past ten years to so drastically change this woman. In order to understand the current Meg, we need to take another quick look at the original Meg.

What do we know about her as a person? Well, the most obvious is that she is the daughter of Madame Giry. She is in the ballet corps of the Opera Populaire. In in Webber's version, her mother is the ballet mistress, who by all accounts is a bit rigid and stern. Little Meg always does what mother says. Perhaps it's that black cane she keeps pounding on the floor.

There is, however, one glaring gap in Meg's life that is never revealed in Webber's version and that is one of a father figure. We are given no indications who her father is, whether he's still alive or dead. In fact, we don't even know if Meg is a legitimate child born in wedlock either—an interesting thought to consider, is it not?

From the point of her holding the mask at the end of the original *Phantom of the Opera*, ten long years have passed. She has continued to do as her mother asked. Meg has followed the Phantom to New York, and for ten years she has supported him along side her mother. Why? Is it because her mother required it of her? She states in *Love Never Dies* that she did as mother bid. Does her motivation go beyond that though?

In my original post about Meg, I call her the woman of possibilities. Even then, it wasn't unreasonable to think that this man who her mother served faithfully for years hadn't produced in Meg some type of deep emotion. What kind of emotions are they though— romantic in nature or fatherly in nature?

In *Love Never Dies*, Meg does everything to get noticed by the Phantom. She has an insatiable desire to please him. She wants to hear the words that were spoken to Christine, "*he is well pleased.*" She wants to shine only for him. She wishes to sing only for him, and she wants him to know something. Know what? That she loves him? She even goes to the extent of giving herself in sexual favors in order to advance the Phantom's career on Coney Island. (*See post note below.*) She desperately wants his favor, but he never sees her sacrifice because he's too busy with his own obsession while Meg is obsessing over him.

When I look at Meg in the version of *Love Never Dies*, I see a woman who is desperate for approval. She's been raised by a stern mother, who no doubt pressured her into being the best. Perhaps she never received enough approval from Madame Giry in her early years. Even now in *Love Never Dies*, she's always asking her mother after her performances how did she do? She's a person with a constant need for affirmation, and it's that flaw in her personality that creates the Meg in *Love Never Dies*.

So what pushes poor Meg over the edge anyway? The number "Bathing Beauty" is the place of no return for Meg. Her unveiling of naked flesh is an outward act of an inward cry. She is exposing herself to such an extent that she thinks the Phantom will finally see her. It's her sly way, perhaps, of upstaging Christine before her aria to show the Phantom she was somehow better. In any case, Meg takes extreme measures to make a point.

What happens, however, is the sad reality that the Phantom wasn't there to see her desperate attempt for approval. Instead, he's with Christine and that puts her over the edge. No longer is the desire for approval the motivation, it's jealousy and despair that shoves Meg down the road to the pier with Gustav and gun in hand.

At the end, we see a Meg lose all control when she's reminded by the Phantom that not everyone can be like Christine. The trigger is pulled, she screams she didn't mean to do it, and her competition dies in the arms of the man she loves. During the ending scene, Meg gathers Christine up in her arms and holds her as the repentant little girl, no doubt looking for forgiveness because all she really wanted was just to be seen.

Do you still think she's just a slut in the story or do you perhaps have an ounce of sympathy for her now? Do people change because of life circumstances and events? The answer, of course, is yes.

As you consider how much Meg Giry has changed from *The Phantom of the Opera*, perhaps you'll see all those tendencies were really buried underneath all along. It was just a matter of circumstances, pressures, and her own desires for acceptance and approval that drove her over the edge of no return.

We all want approval from those we love—whether it's from a parent, friend, boyfriend, or spouse. She's like anybody else crying on the inside for someone to tell her they care. In reality, her cry isn't much different than the Phantom's in Leroux.

"*All I ever wanted was to be loved for myself.*"

(POSTED FRIDAY, APRIL 2, 2010)

POST NOTE: MEG TURNING SEXUAL FAVORS IN THIS VERSION CAN BE UPSETTING, BUT IN REALITY DURING THE LATE NINETEENTH CENTURY, ESPECIALLY IN THE WORLD OF PARIS OPERA, THOSE THAT PERFORMED OFTEN DID "SERVICE" PATRONS. THE MORALS OF THE DAY WERE QUITE DIFFERENT. MOST FEMALE PERFORMERS WERE CONSIDERED MORALLY LOOSE AND AKIN TO PROSTITUTES. IF WE ARE TO PORTRAY THE ACTUALITY OF THE DAY, IT WOULDN'T BE UNREASONABLE TO THINK THAT MEG WAS AWARE OF THAT practice back in Paris and hence used it in her new role on Coney Island to further along the Phantom's success. Whether it's right or wrong or you like it or not, it was merely a fact of history.

Gustav in LND

"It is a wise father that knows his own child."
William Shakespeare

Who is Gustav? Don't recognize the name from the original story? Well, he's a new character and a new dimension inserted into *Love Never Dies*. After his mother perishes, he takes her place and gives to his father another chance for redemption through a simple hug of acceptance.

I will say that the young men who played Gustav on stage in London were a joy to watch. They were fearless and talented children around the age of twelve. Seven individuals rotated playing the role in the original London cast, and many more followed until it closed at the Adelphi. They sang with Christine, kept up with the wild and loud choreographed "The Beauty Underneath" and brought us to tears at the critical moments before the curtain came down.

Gustav is the son of Christine and Erik, though originally Raoul believes the boy to be his. You have this sneaking suspicion that Raoul hasn't bonded with Gustav as his short temper is even displayed toward the "boy" as he calls him. Obviously, he is closer to his mother, who appears to protect him from Raoul's anger. Not until Erik puts two and two together, since the boy has a gift for music, does his real identity come forth.

Christine admits the truth, but Gustav is still protected from the knowledge of his real father until the end. Raoul, of course, discovers the possibility during "Devil Takes the Hindmost" when the Phantom insinuates that Gustav is his child instead.

In the rocking beauty underneath song, Erik rejoices in their similarities until he shows his son what is behind the mask. In shock, Gustav screams and runs away, leaving Erik devastated.

It's not until the end of *Love Never Dies* when Christine during her final moments before death tells Gustav the truth. After the emotional death scene, Gustav takes over the role his mother. Standing before his father, he removes the Phantom's mask and then embraces him in unconditional love. Needless to say the scene has the tendency to make your eyes water.

As I mentioned in my post about The Phantom in *Love Never Dies,* Gustav's name suggests that he is indeed the one who from this point forward leads his father into a new life. What happens from here on out is probably a good place to ponder. The curtain comes down, the show is over, and you are left to wonder if any good follows after the horrific tragedy plays out. What do you think?

(WRITTEN FOR THE 3RD EDITION)

Conclusion

"He let me go at last . . . closed the door and left me alone to my reflections."

I hope you have enjoyed my down-to-earth fan review of the characters, emotions, symbols, and places/things in this timeless masterpiece. "The Music of the Night" never ends. Every single day people stumble across my blog from around the world, all driven by simple Internet searches on some aspect of the story. *The Phantom of the Opera* is an immortal tale that profoundly touches hearts. Frankly, it amazes me.

My blog/book is by no means meant to be a scholarly review of the story in its three forms (book, stage, and movie). In contrast, I have focused on the elementary aspects of the tale that include character motivations, emotions, and symbols sprinkled throughout. For more in-depth scholarly review on the original *The Phantom of the Opera*, I suggest you look elsewhere.

I sincerely want to thank all of my readers, especially those who have been faithful to my blog throughout my journey and encouraged me to put my posts into book form. The many comments left on my blog and emails that I have received are a tremendous blessing to me. They also are proof that this story touches and speaks to fans in multiple ways.

Again, thanks for letting me share with you *Lessons from the Phantom of the Opera*. It's time to close the door now and leave you to your reflections.

Endnotes

[1](Author Unknown) The Bigger Picture – "'Phantom' A Fairy Tale for Modern Women; Fatal Attraction or Final Liberation?" Retrieved February 1, 2008 from: http://www.ratherronge.co.za

[2]Bernice H. Hill "Reflections on The Phantom of the Opera" Retrieved January 26, 2008 from: http://www.cgjungpage.org

[3]Kobberstad, Jakob N. Norsk læsebog Kra: Aschehoug, 1882, Vol. 2.

[4]Fitz-Randolph, M. H. (2009, July 29). What is the Persona in Jungian Psychology. Suite101.com. Retrieved February 9, 2009 from: http://clinical-psychology.suite101.com

[5]William Congreve, The Mourning Bride, Act 1 Scene 1, English dramatist (1670 - 1729)

[6]Edgar Allan Poe "The Masque of the Red Death" Free Public Domain Books from the Classic Literature Library. Retrieved from: http://www.classicliterature.co.uk

[7]With courtesy of Comté Cocteau Paris, France http://jeancocteau.net

[8]Banham, Martin, ed. (1998), The Cambridge Guide to Theatre, Cambridge: Cambridge UP.

About the Author

Vicki Hopkins is an award-winning and Amazon bestselling author. Her usual genre is historical fiction (family saga) and historical romance. However, she also writes contemporary and historical romantic suspense under two other pen names. She has written nine fiction novels.

With Russian blood on her father's side and English on her mother's, she blames her ancestors for the lethal combination in her genes that influence her stories. Tragedy and drama might be found between her pages, but she eventually gives her readers a happy ending.

She lives in the beautiful, but rainy, Pacific Northwest with a pesky cat who refuses to let her sleep in. Her hobbies include researching her English ancestry, traveling to England when she can afford it, and plotting her next book.

In July of 2010, Vicki released her own exciting Phantom of the Opera sequel entitled, *The Phantom of Valletta*. The book has been well received in the Phantom community and from readers on the isle of Malta, where it was featured in *The Malta Sunday Times* in August of 2010.

For more information visit: _The Phantom of Valletta_

You can find updates on Vicki's future releases on her author website at Vicki Hopkins, Author.

You may follow Vicki at:
Email: vicki@vickihopkins.com
Twitter: http://twitter.com/VHopkins_Author
Facebook: http://www.facebook.com/Vicki.Hopkins.Author

www.ingramcontent.com/pod-product-compliance
Lightning Source LLC
Chambersburg PA
CBHW031244290426
44109CB00012B/421